"Moving to Nowhere"

864-3008
Doris

"Moving to Nowhere"

Children's Stories of Homelessness

Mary E. Walsh

Auburn House

New York • Westport, Connecticut • London

Library of Congress Cataloging-in-Publication Data

Walsh, Mary E. (Mary Elizabeth).
    Moving to nowhere : children's stories of homelessness / Mary E. Walsh.
      p. cm.
    Includes bibliographical references and index.
    ISBN 0–86569–017–0 (alk. paper).—ISBN 0–86569–202–5 (pbk. : alk. paper)
    1. Homeless children—United States. 2. Homelessness—United States. I. Title.
    HV4505.W257 1992
    362.7'08'6942—dc20   91–34709

British Library Cataloguing in Publication Data is available.

Library of Congress Catalog Card Number: 91–34709
ISBN: 0–86569–017–0 (hc)
ISBN: 0–86569–202–5 (pb)

First published in 1992

Auburn House, 88 Post Road West, Westport, CT 06881
An imprint of Greenwood Publishing Group, Inc.

Printed in the United States of America

The paper used in this book complies with the Permanent Paper Standard issued by the National Information Standards Organization (Z39.48–1984).

10 9 8 7 6 5 4 3 2 1

To children everywhere who are without a home,
to their parents who struggle to find one,
and to the tireless human service professionals
who, in spite of difficult and often cynical times,
have not given up on the value of helping those in need.

Contents

Preface

In nearly twenty years as a clinical-developmental psychologist, particularly in my position in the Department of Family and Community Medicine at University of Massachusetts Medical School, I have had the privilege of working with poor children and their families. Most of these families lived in the inner city, struggling to survive in substandard housing on minimum income. I have seen these children and families in neighborhood health centers, schools, hospitals, and other community programs. While some of my work with these families has involved empirical research, much of it has been clinical in nature. As they related their day-to-day struggles to have what so many of them describe as "a good life," I have increasingly come to appreciate the profound effects of poverty, particularly on the lives of the children.

In their efforts to make me understand, these children told me their stories—stories that I gradually came to realize had a depth and richness far beyond the limits of psychological measures. In a simple and elegant way they told me what they felt about their lives, their struggles, their hopes, and their dreams.

Nearly five years ago, when I began to work with mothers and children who were homeless, I heard variants on these same stories. The pain was sharper, the hopes more dimmed, and the dreams a little further out of reach. The stories of these voiceless children greatly affected me. I learned how much I did not know about their lives. In order to enable them to tell their story to others, I recorded their narratives and present them in this book.

In bringing this project to completion I am indebted to many people. The staff members of the many shelters I visited, while always protective of the privacy of their shelter guests, understood my purpose. The obvious support they gave me made it easier for the children to come to trust me.

Boston College provided me with the time, financial resources, and moral support to do what it believed was important work. Without this assistance, the project could not have been accomplished.

My colleagues in psychology, particularly Dr. Roger Bibace, have taught me many times over how to make meaning out of our discipline by using it to serve those in need.

My research assistant, Maureen Buckley, a doctoral student in counseling psychology, spent an extraordinary number of hours transcribing tapes, sharpening ideas, and hearing the tiniest of these children's voices.

My husband, Dan, who has had a lifelong commitment to working with children and families living in poverty, has supported and inspired every step of this project.

It would be presumptuous of me to thank the children who told me their stories. I serve only to bring their voices to a wider audience. They can and do speak for themselves.

"Moving to Nowhere"

Chapter One

Introduction

Widespread family homelessness is a recent phenomenon in the United States. In the last decade the number of homeless families has increased dramatically. Because the phenomenon is relatively new, most helping professionals—psychologists, teachers, social workers, nurses, and doctors—have had little opportunity to learn about homelessness before meeting homeless children and their families. The purpose of this book is to provide a glimpse into the world of homeless children so that helping professionals may reach out more quickly and effectively to ease the burdens of these children and families. The view of homelessness presented here will be that provided by the children themselves through the stories they tell about their lives.

Human service providers have long been aware that the most critical ingredient in helping another person is an understanding of where that person is coming from. At its essence, a helping relationship requires that the helper know how the other person makes meaning out of his or her world of experiences. While they can never completely enter into the mind of the other, effective helpers are continually moving in the direction of "seeing what the other sees." It is this perspective that constitutes the basis of empathy and ultimately leads to the empowerment of people to make positive and productive choices in their lives.

The meaning that a person makes out of the people, places, and events encountered in life is most clearly heard in the story that the person tells about himself or herself. Developmental psychologists have long taken the position that the making of meaning, or what Bruner (1990) recently referred to as "world making," is a "principal function of the mind." Adults and children are continually about the business of constructing their world, sorting it out, and making sense out of all the pieces in their lives. In constructing their life stories, they are "authors," as Bakhtin would have it (Bruner, 1990).

Telling one's story is in a real sense "making one's life." It is through stories that those who listen come to know how others have made meaning, what their world looks like from their point of view. Stories are a clear and simple way for one to see as the other sees. Through the stories of homelessness told here, it is hoped that helping professionals can come to understand the world of homeless children, and ultimately, through understanding their world, support and enable them on their journey to adulthood.

FAMILY HOMELESSNESS

To what can the recent rise in homelessness among families be attributed? It is clear that the fundamental causes are poverty and a severe shortage of affordable housing. Homeless families, whether on welfare or working for the minimum wage, spend an excessive proportion of their income for housing. In addition, the number of low-income housing units is decreasing annually. In the context of insufficient money and housing, poor families in the United States today are confronted by numerous other problems: under- and unemployment, social disaffiliation, family and street violence, substance abuse, cutbacks in the availability of social services, and the decline of the traditional nuclear family. It is against the backdrop of some or many of these problems that poor families struggle, not only to maintain themselves physically, but also to survive psychologically, as families. In spite of their efforts, some families eventually fall through the not-so-safe "safety nets" and become homeless.

Regardless of the varied causes of the general phenomenon of homelessness, individual homeless families differ significantly from one another in terms of how homelessness happened to them. Homelessness is a term that includes a wide variety of people and circumstances. On the surface, what this diverse population of people share is the lack of a roof over their heads, but the crisis of finding oneself without a home can take several different forms. In their research comparing homeless families with housed public assistance families in New York, Weitzman, Knickman, and Shinn (1990) distinguished three common pathways into homelessness.

The first pathway was characterized by a sudden move from a stable housing situation to homelessness (43% of the sample). Loss of status as a primary tenant and subsequent homelessness was attributed primarily to eviction or rent difficulties. Many of these families were paying rents that exceeded their public assistance shelter allowance, living in apartments on the open housing market rather than low-income projects or subsidized apartments. While these families had relatively stable housing prior to their homelessness, their housing situations had also been characterized by difficulties such as overcrowding, prior history of eviction, and substantial structural problems in the residences. Interpersonal difficulties with or physical abuse by spouses or boyfriends also contributed to homelessness.

In contrast to the rapid descent into homelessness, Weitzman and her colleagues also distinguished a pathway in which homelessness was the culmination of a "slow slide" from stable housing to an increasingly unstable living situation. This characterized only 13 percent of the sample. Although once stable tenants, two-thirds of these individuals had left their last permanent housing one or more years ago. In the years after losing stable housing, these families had existed in crowded, doubled-up conditions. Over half of these families did not contribute rent to the families with whom they doubled up; in 60 percent of the cases, conflict with the primary tenants was cited as the reason for leaving. This group had an average of over three moves in the past three years and, compared with the other two homeless groups, had experienced more problems and more difficult life conditions. A small portion of these families had experience with psychiatric hospitalization, detoxification programs, or child protective services.

A third pathway characterized those individuals who had never maintained independent housing for a period of one year or longer. This group comprised 44 percent of those studied. The pattern was typical for small families headed by young mothers who had never been on their own. The majority had lived with parents or other family members, with a large number making little or no contribution to rent. Almost immediately after these living arrangements fell through, these families moved into the shelters, never establishing independence.

RESEARCH ON HOMELESS FAMILIES

In an attempt to learn about their experiences and their needs, and to determine more effective directions for social policy, homeless families have increasingly become a focus of empirical research. Some of this research has looked at the nature and extent of homelessness. Statistics on the number of homeless families are difficult to formulate, due to varying definitions of homelessness as well as the transient nature of the population. Nevertheless, it has been estimated that families make up one-third of the total homeless population and that children contribute to over half of this group (Reyes and Waxman, 1986). Estimates range from 30,000 to 500,000 children who are homeless with their parents (Children's Defense Fund, 1988). On any given night, 100,000 children are homeless across the country. The majority of these homeless children are under five years of age (Bassuk, Rubin, and Lauriat, 1986).

A significant amount of research has been directed at describing homeless families. While most homeless families are headed by a single mother, the composition of these families appears to vary from one region of the country to the other (Bassuk, 1990). The average age of the mothers is twenty-seven years. The mothers are likely not to have completed their high school education, and have limited work skills. Many have relied on Aid to Families with Dependent Children (AFDC) benefits for a period of years.

When compared with poor housed mothers, mothers in homeless families appear to have more limited social supports, that is, fewer relationships with people—family or friends—on whom they can rely (Bassuk, Rubin, and Lauriat, 1986). In addition, the men with whom these mothers have relationships are more likely to have poor work histories, as well as more alcohol and substance abuse problems than the men with whom housed women establish relationships (Bassuk and Rosenberg, 1988). A number of homeless mothers report having been battered in their relationships with men and to have been victims of physical and sexual abuse when they were children (Bassuk and Rosenberg, 1988). While the prevalence of addictions among homeless mothers has not been systematically documented, Weinreb and Bassuk (1990) note that, according to service providers connected with inner cities nationwide, many shelter dwellers are abusing drugs, particularly alcohol and "crack."

Compared to poor housed mothers, homeless mothers have moved more frequently and have lived alone less often (Bassuk and Rosenberg, 1988). In addition, homeless mothers have been found to have less education than homeless men and women who are single, with only 43 percent having obtained at least a high school degree (Burt and Cohen, 1989). This stands in contrast to the 81 percent of U.S. adults and 57 percent of poor U.S. adults who have graduated from high school (Bureau of the Census, 1985).

RESEARCH ON HOMELESS CHILDREN

Empirical research has also addressed the effects of homelessness on children. As members of the fastest-growing segment of the homeless population (Waxman and Reyes, 1989), homeless children are faced with serious disruption in their growth and development. Impediments faced by these children may include inadequate stimulation, lack of consistency and stability, insufficient peer interaction, and problems satisfying basic needs, such as food, safety and shelter. Homeless children are subjected to various educational, developmental, socio-emotional and behavioral problems. While a majority of these difficulties are similar to those facing housed children, the specific circumstance of homelessness exacerbates the possibility of their occurring, while simultaneously making it less likely that such problems will be detected and adequately addressed. What may be a minor and easily treatable problem for children in more stable circumstances may develop into a major difficulty for homeless children.

A 1985 study comparing homeless and poor housed mothers and their children revealed that 54 percent of homeless preschoolers displayed one major developmental delay, in contrast to 16 percent of housed preschoolers (Bassuk and Rosenberg, 1988). Language delays constituted 37 percent of the developmental delays cited. Thirty-four percent were unable to perform crucial personal and social developmental tasks. In addition, 18 percent had deficits in gross motor skills and 15 percent exhibited delays in fine motor coordination.

The risk of developmental delay is heightened prenatally by factors such as genetics, maternal illness, inadequate nutrition, lack of prenatal care, and exposure to drugs or alcohol. One study encompassing four hundred pregnant women in New York welfare hotels found that over 39 percent had received no prenatal care (Chavkin, Kristal, Seabron, and Guigli, 1987).

Homeless preschoolers also exhibit behavioral difficulties. Studies have pointed to problems with attention, sleep, shyness, speech, withdrawal and aggression, regressive behaviors, inappropriate, overly friendly social interactions with adults, immature peer interactions, and food issues, such as hunger and hoarding (Bassuk, Rubin, and Lauriat, 1986; Molnar, 1988).

Socio-emotional development in school-aged children has also been found to suffer as a result of homelessness. Compared with their housed peers, homeless children displayed markedly more shyness, aggression, withdrawal, dependence, demanding behaviors, and attentional difficulties (Bassuk, Rubin, and Lauriat, 1986). As reported by Bassuk and Rosenberg (1988), more homeless children over five years of age evidenced clinical levels of depression and anxiety than housed children. In the opinions of their mothers, 41 percent of homeless children, in contrast to 23 percent of housed children, were currently failing or performing at a below average level in school. Other researchers have found that homeless children are experiencing similar difficulties in the realms of self-esteem, anxiety, depression, and stress (Waxman and Reyes, 1987).

Homelessness has been found to have a profoundly negative effect on the cognitive development and educational progress of homeless children. Obtaining an education, an everyday component of most children's lives, is typically fraught with difficulties for homeless children. Frequent moves create inconsistencies in the schooling of these children. Trouble with paperwork or other access-related issues, lack of transportation or clothing, and chronic health problems are only some of the myriad of factors that cause homeless children to miss a significant amount of schooling. It has been reported that 43 percent of school-aged homeless children are not attending school at all, and that 30 percent of those who are in school fall at least one grade behind their peers (Hall and Maza, 1990).

Homeless children are more likely to have been retained, to be receiving special education services, and to be behind their classmates academically (Bassuk and Rubin, 1987). As reported by their parents, 19 percent were viewed as having developed learning disabilities as a consequence of their homelessness (Colorado Children's Campaign, 1987). Rafferty and Rollins (1989) examined the influence of homelessness on education, focusing on homeless children in the New York City area. They found that becoming homeless results in a considerable amount of "bouncing" around. Sixty-six percent of the families studied had lived in at least two shelters and 29 percent had been in at least four. They found that most children transferred schools upon becoming homeless, with 33 percent having transferred between two and six times. The more frequently facilities were changed, the more disruptions in the children's school experience. Despite legislation such as the Stewart B. McKinney Homeless Assistance Act (Public Law 100-77) allowing children to attend their former or local school with free transportation, many parents were uninformed about their rights.

Social, emotional, and cognitive developmental problems are exacerbated by a variety of health care issues. Access to health care remains a problem for these children. Lack of health insurance, transportation problems, distrust of official personnel, and discontinuity of health care all contribute to the health problems of homeless children. Studies have shown that homeless children have twice the rate of chronic illness and suffer from a greater number of acute problems than their housed counterparts (Wright and Weber, 1987; Miller and Lin, 1988). One report indicated that there is a greater incidence of upper respiratory infection among homeless children, and attributed this to exposure to the elements and unsuitable living conditions (Roberts and Henry, 1986). Limited or no access to cooking facilities, inability to pay for food, and inadequacy of supplemental food programs provide obstacles for obtaining proper nutrition. Other health risks include poor sleeping accommodations, inadequate clothing, and insufficient provisions for daily hygiene.

Overall, the empirical studies of the past decade have yielded important and disturbing findings: the effects of homelessness on its young victims are profound and devastating. Standardized measures of cognitive and socio-emotional development have demonstrated clearly that depression, anxiety, developmental delay, and school failure are but a few of the many consequences of homelessness for children.

VOICES OF HOMELESS CHILDREN

While this body of empirical research is critical in terms of informing public policy decisions—that is, providing the political decision makers with incontrovertible evidence of the destructive consequences of homelessness—it is of more limited use to the frontline service providers and clinicians who, in order to help these children, must understand their worlds. To describe a child as depressed or anxious does not fully capture the reality of the homeless child. Summarizing the child's experience by means of a quantitative score on a depression inventory does little to illuminate the condition and experience of an individual homeless child. The clinician, in order to be truly helpful, must have some understanding of the child's world. The clinician must know not only the objective facts of a situation, but also how the child experiences these realities. The most direct way to come to know how homeless children make meaning out of their world is simply to ask them to tell their story, and, as Coles would have it, "to listen carefully, record faithfully, comprehend as fully as possible" (Coles, 1989, p. 25).

The purpose of this book is to allow homeless children, through their stories, to speak for themselves. The voices of the children presented here tell of the effects of homelessness with data that is raw and exquisitely compelling. It is not the data represented by the shorthand of statistics, and thus does not shortchange the lives of these children.

This project grew out of my earlier experience working with homeless children. As a researcher, my initial efforts were directed at assessing the level of self-esteem in these children. Using a standardized measure, I examined preschool and school-aged homeless children's self-concepts in the domains of academic, social, and athletic competence, physical appearance, and behavioral conduct. The findings confirmed what I had anticipated, that the self-concepts of homeless children had been battered by their experiences.

After completing the study, however, I was intensely bothered by all of the data that these children had offered to me that I simply could not look at in my study. In the process of "filling out the forms," these children had told me their stories—stories that were significantly richer than their scores on the standardized measure. The statistics of the empirical study reflected only a piece of their lives, while the words and feelings of the narratives seemed to tell almost all. As a clinician, I recognized that it was the stories that would give me the insights necessary to help these children.

This research experience heightened in me the inevitable tension between the scientific and clinical approaches to understanding human behavior. When the goal is knowledge, the group means or average scores yielded by the scientific method provide critical and significant information. When the goal is helping, however, the focus must be the individual, not only the group, and the data must be the meaning the individual makes out of his or her world, not only the average score of the group into which he or she is classified (Bibace and Walsh, 1979; 1981). These children taught me, not only about homelessness, but also about psychology, for I learned from them the critical importance of doing research that allows the human voice to be heard.

It was not only the absence of statistics, but also the modification of common research practice that made this effort different from the more traditional approaches. At the level of the individual child, the stories I heard made an immediate demand on me as a clinical psychologist. I did not always stay neutral in my response. There were many interviews in which, after hearing a tale of pain, I did engage in some therapeutic activity as a human and professional response. At the end of the child's story, we talked, the child and I, about ways of dealing with the circumstances that might lessen the hurt. We spoke of alternative strategies for surviving on a day-to-day basis.

At the broader level of the group, I also felt compelled to respond in a nontraditional way. Traditionally, researchers test subjects in one or another setting, express their gratitude to the subjects and staff, and move on. The researchers take, and the subjects of the research give. Mutuality is assumed to exist at another level, in that the particular population will ultimately benefit from the participation of the sample group in the research. In the context of homelessness, this traditional response seemed too distant. In some partial return for the willingness of these children, families, and shelter staff to help me, I offered to assist the shelter in some concrete way. Most accepted the offer and asked for assistance with staff workshops, preschool developmental screening, or advocacy at the level of local or state government on behalf of the needs of homeless families.

For the core of this project, I invited fifty-five homeless children, ranging in age from four to eighteen years, to tell me their stories. With the permission of the children and their parents, I recorded the stories of how they became homeless, what homelessness was like for them, how they manage on a day-to-day basis, and their hopes and dreams for the future. Each of these children provided on average approximately one and one-half to two hours of taped conversations.

These children lived in nearly twenty different community shelters and welfare motels or hotels, which, for purposes of this volume, will all be referred to as shelters. The shelters were located in the Northeast, mostly in urban areas. The conversations were conducted in the shelter in a room that the shelter director or staff designated. Typically, the room was a space that was not in use at that moment and that was private, for example, an available staff office or a play room. In no case did children tell their story in the presence of other people. On a few occasions, mothers invited me to use the family's room at the shelter while the mother and other children waited in another part of the building.

Each of the children I spoke with was told the reasons for the conversations. In all cases, parents were provided both a verbal and written description of the study and were assured that any identifying characteristics would not be reported. They gave their consent in writing. Additionally, children were provided with a verbal description of the study and gave verbal consent. A small number of children chose not to participate.

Children were told that they were free to leave the conversation at any time, could talk about what they wanted and only what they wanted. They were assured that their identity would be protected. For this reason, any identifying data such as name, geographic location, and family composition, has been altered to protect the anonymity of the children and their families.

In listening to these stories, I felt both pain and privilege. By inviting people to share their story, a researcher is asking to hear the raw truth. The protection from pain afforded by the more sanitized, standardized pencil and paper measures simply does not exist. In the course of this project, there were moments and days when I felt the only reasonable response to the intense pain of these children was to put aside the research objective and simply provide whatever therapeutic intervention I could. I was kept at my task by the hope that the stories of these children would assist other helping professionals to work with other homeless children.

While difficult, my listening to and recording these stories was, simultaneously, an extraordinary privilege. These children trusted me with some of their most private thoughts and feelings. They spoke candidly of their hopes, their disappointments, their worries, and their dreams. They showed me their toys, they shared a joke, and they made me understand. These children, each in his or her own way, seared their stories into my soul. I continue to hear their voices and see their faces, and I find myself continually wondering about where they are and how they are doing.

This book contains the stories of twenty children in their near entirety. Repetition, either in the child's story or in its use in the book, as well as some extraneous conversation, constitute the reasons for any gaps, which are indicated by ellipses. Otherwise, the stories are as the children told them. The commentary that accompanies their stories is meant to amplify their voices as well as speak for the thirty-five other homeless children with whom I spoke, whose entire stories could not be included due to lack of space.

In their stories, the children raise many important themes. In order to present these stories in some coherent manner, I have taken the liberty of grouping these stories into the themes as I heard them. The two stories presented at the beginning of each chapter were selected because they highlighted the theme in some special way. However, it should be noted that the selected stories are not confined to that theme. The issues raised by these children include their understanding and explanation to themselves of why they became homeless, and their experience of life in the shelter or motel. In their stories, the children describe their experience with peers and with significant adults such as teachers. These children talk about their families and their day-to-day lives. They relate their fears and uncertainties, their strategies for survival, and their hopes and dreams for the future.

What are recorded here are stories of homeless children. But they are, at the same time, more general stories of people who struggle and hope for a better future. And, in this sense, they reflect the human story—a story of which each of us has our unique version. In listening to these stories and sharing them in this volume, I am mindful of what the family doctor and writer William Carlos Williams told his student, Robert Coles, many years ago: "Their story, yours, mine—it's what we carry with us on this trip we take, and we owe it to each other to respect our stories and learn from them" (Coles, 1989, p. 30).

Chapter Two

"Nowhere Else to Go": Becoming Homeless

INGRID

*Ingrid is a nine-year-old third-grader. Her family consists of T. J.,
Elizabeth, Ellen, Ethan, and Chris, as well as their mother. The
children range in age from one to seventeen years. They have been
in the shelter for five months. They have not lived in a shelter before.
Until several years ago their mother was working two jobs and
receiving child support from her ex-husband, the father of the oldest
three children. She became involved with a man who became
Ethan's and Ellen's father. After they broke up, she was reunited
with her ex-husband. They had a daughter together, but soon after,
her husband left again and she found herself overwhelmed by bills.
She received no help from her ex-husband, who was paying child
support to two other women and their children. She fell behind in
rent and went to welfare for help. This agency said that she could
only obtain assistance if she had received an eviction notice from
the court. When she obtained this, the family moved into the shelter.*

I'm 9 years old and my sister's Elizabeth and my brother's T. J. I
think we moved into this shelter in January and it's November now. It's
been a long time. It's a pretty good place though. Usually I like it when
I play out in the yard. We have a big swing set and usually that's what
I usually do every day. Or I ride my bike. What I don't like here is

when I have to go to bed early on weekends. I think it's a good place, though.

We came here because we had a house on Briarwood Road that was down in Seton. It cost too much money, and my mom couldn't pay for all the stuff so that we had to move out and then we had to move into here. On November 30th we'll be moving to Loville. I don't really want to go to Loville because almost all my friends are down in Seton. But I'll probably meet some more friends. I'll be going to Fillmore school. Last year I went to Briarwood School. I'm at North Seton School now. When I was in kindergarten I went to William Smith School. Then when I was in the first grade until second grade I was in Briarwood. I stayed back two times. And so I've been to Briarwood for three years. And this is probably my first year being at North Seton. So I'm going to be there half a year and then I'm going to Fillmore in Loville. . . .

Living here, it's partly not good. When my mom didn't have enough money for where we were living and we had to move, I thought we would be moving to Loville or something like that but we really moved to North Seton. I thought we were going to be moving to a house, but it was a shelter. I knew before we came that it was going to be a shelter. My mother told me. I was surprised. I felt funny about it because when we came here to the shelter, we went downstairs and everybody was crowding around to see us. They wanted to see because they didn't get to see us yet and they wanted to talk to us.

I asked Mom why we didn't go to a house, and she said because sometimes she's broke and sometimes she's not. Sometimes she has lots of money, and sometimes she doesn't. She gets broke because usually all the time she has to pay for all the bills and all that stuff so she can't pay for all the other stuff. So sometimes she runs out of money. And then she has to borrow, then she has to pay it back. When she runs out of money sometimes I feel sad because if we run out of food and she doesn't have any money, then we won't have anything to eat. Sometimes we don't have enough food. But partly all the time she goes shopping every week. Sometimes I worry that we won't have enough food, sometimes. It's scary. . . .

Sometimes I tell my worries to my friend Joanna. She's from a far away place. And one friend is Alison and one of them is Mia, and Johnny. Brian doesn't really know I live in a shelter because Joanna's known me since second grade that's all. She's only known me for two years. When she heard that I was living in a shelter, she didn't say much. She just talked to me a lot. Sometimes I don't like living in the shelter 'cause fire alarms go off. Once it went off at five o'clock in the morning. And once it went off because a spider was stuck in it and another time it was because my mom was cooking breakfast and the fire alarm went off. Oh brother. That was hard. That was very hard.

Sometimes I just think that my friends think that I'm poor and they're rich. I think that's right. But it depends because usually everybody almost doesn't have money and then they work a lot and they get lots of money. So, I don't think they're rich. They have to work for their money. When they say that to me, I feel bad. Sometimes I think "We live in a shelter and everybody says that we're poor." Being poor is bad. Sometimes when you're poor you can't pay the bills. If you don't pay the bills and stuff, you'll have to move out or something and you might live on the street. Sometimes I worry that we'll live on the street. But tomorrow in school, I can bring food cans, but not anything that will rot easily. Because they're going to be collecting them in school for poor people for Thanksgiving. It's not for us, it's just for our school. We have to bring them in, because we have lots of vegetables and soup cans and all that stuff in the cabinet at this shelter. So we can give it to people who are poor. Somebody just comes around school with big boxes and you put it in. When they start collecting food for the poor in school, sometimes I feel like I'm poor. I feel bad about it. It makes me feel sad. Once on a commercial I saw a lady and she had two children, a baby and about a four-year-old, and they were just sitting on a street crying. They were crying because they didn't have any food or anything and they were starving. Sometimes I have bad dreams about it. Usually sometimes when I'm sleeping I just, I just think of it and I just wake up and then I just think about it and then go back to sleep. I just think about when my mom doesn't have any more money and we might have to stay in the shelter for a long time. I worry about it. Sometimes I can't remember my bad dreams. It's real hard to be poor sometimes.

There's a girl in my classroom named Elizabeth and she was in a shelter too. She lives in one right now. I know because I was in the classroom one day and she asked me if I lived in a house or a shelter and I said "A shelter" and she said "I do, too." She said she doesn't really like it either. She doesn't like living in a shelter. She likes it better in a house. I do too. Because in a shelter sometimes you don't really get to do anything. In a house, you have a lot of rooms. In the shelter, we only have a little room. We only have a small room. And then when I get my own house, I get to get my own room and I don't have to share it with everybody. I don't like sharing because when we lived in Briarwood Road we had five rooms, but my mom couldn't fit any of our old things anywhere, and so she had to make one of the rooms a storage room. So I had to share one of the rooms with Chris and Ellen and my sister had to share one with Ethan. And my mom had to share it with my other brother because there weren't enough. I want my own room. When we get a house, me and my sister get our own room. And the baby has to share with my mom and T. J. gets his own room. The new house we're going to is better because it has four floors and it's a real big house. I saw it. I went inside of it. I like it. It's just going to a new school that I don't like. But, it will be a nice house.

We're going to get furniture. My grandmother went up to Washington and she's going to sell her house and she's going to be moving somewhere, I forget the name of it, and then she's told my mom she'd give her some furniture and a table set stuff. And my mom's going to buy the beds. When we moved in here we had to put our stuff in storage. But I brought some of my favorite things here, like I brought some of my books and things I color with and some games. But I still miss my other stuff because in my other stuff I used to have Barbies and me and my sister used to have lots of games and we used to play with lots of things when we lived in Briarwood Road. I liked Briarwood Road. And there was a lot of friends that we played with. I miss my friends.

Thanksgiving is next week. I think my mom's going to cook lots of things for Thanksgiving and we'll probably have it here at the shelter. It'll be a special party and that will be good.

TARA

Tara, her four-year-old sister, three-year-old brother, and her mother moved a considerable distance to come to the present area. The move was precipitated by an argument between her mother and father. Her mother left the father, selling all that they had and borrowing money for bus fare to come to their present location. After arriving, they stayed with her sister for two weeks until the landlord complained that the apartment was too crowded. They are now hoping to go back to their original state of residence.

I'm nine years old and I'm in the second grade. I've been here eight months in this state and living in Southfield House for seven months. Before that I was in Florida. That's where I always lived. I was living with my sister and brother and my mother and father. And then we decided to come here. It's a long story.

This one time, my mother and father got in a big fight over money and then my friend Bernadette was over my house and my parents kept on screaming and yelling and hitting and crying, and kicking and everything. We could hear screeches all over the house, because my mother and father were having a fight. And then when my mother came out she said to my father "Thank you, a-hole for screwing up our lives" and then he slammed the door and then he got in the car . . . walked out and didn't come back! . . . My mom went out. I don't know where she went. But she said that she was going out for the night because she was really mad and then my dad came in. He busted the door, then he walked in, grabbed us. . . . And then he brought us to the girl Nancy's house and her and her husband, Gary, did drugs and they sell drugs, and so he brought us over there and then my mother called and she said 'I'm coming to get them now.' . . . Then my mother got there and I was putting Crystal in the car and my dad's favorite was Adam, and he's four, and my dad said he was going to put him in the car, so my mother got in the car and was waiting but then he didn't put him in. . . . Then my dad pushed my mother down because he didn't want her to get Adam and then she jumped right back up again, trying to get Adam and then Nancy got in the way.

And then my mother pushed her shoulder and Gary came out and he was so crazy he just threw my mother up against the car. We could hear the big bang and then he threw her up against the car and starts strangling her and we could hear her trying to gasp for air and then my dad has to pry Gary's hands off my mother and then her neck was all red. She went to the police and then they said she couldn't do anything about it and her neck was the evidence. And then we came out. And then Bernadette thought it was her fault and she left. Just because she was there. I know whose fault it was. My father's. Then my mother took us back. She finally got Adam that night and then we went to Emily's house, her friend, and then we stayed over. . . .

We were with Emily in Florida and then we were going to fly back to here, but then my aunt's Visa card was disconnected or something. And then we couldn't fly back, we had to take the bus! We needed her card, because she was going to pay for us. The card was disconnected. And so she couldn't give us the money to get on the plane. And then we had to take a bus. We got the money for the bus from Emily, my mother's friend. We came to this state because my mother's sister's out here and a lot of people we know are out here. Our furniture at home in Florida all got selled. I was there when it got selled. When I saw it being selled I was sad because all these memories were getting selled. Like, the car and the couch, the TV, the clothes, the dresser, the bed, everything, even my clothes. A lot of memories were in those things that got sold.

The only thing I brought on the bus was some clothes, not all of them because we had too much. The bus ride was dumb. Dumb is what was dumb about it. Just plain dumb! We had to sleep on the stupid bus! With a boy, where there was a guy, he took up three seats, and all he would do all night was lay down and fart, all night, so nobody could sleep. And he did it on purpose too. He stunk up the whole bus. We were on the bus three and a half days. All day on the bus all we did is just ride. We didn't play any games or anything, just ride.

I hate this shelter. They have rats, they have cockroaches, they have mice. I've seen them. They have only one rat next door. They have rats, mice, cockroaches, flying cockroaches. This place is a disaster. Mice are in our room, cockroaches. We know they're there because we caught one on the glue trap, wiggling around. What I don't like about the shelter is everything. Like Jackie. She's mean. She says mean things to me. I don't like Susan Hunter either. I don't like anybody that works here. Except Marie and Ginger. I like Ginger. And Alice and Josephine. I really like Alice.

So, we came on that bus, and got off the bus, and first we stayed at my aunt's. And then we came here to the shelter. We couldn't stay at my aunt's because she was getting kicked out because we were there. There were too many people. My aunt knew about this place. . . . So my mom told me that we were going to go to a shelter. But she didn't tell me where it was going to be. And I didn't even know what it was going to be like. I didn't even know what a shelter was except all people who have no place to go, that's where they go! . . . I just thought it was like something where all the stores were and there was a big glass part in the middle. That's the shelter, like it's a square. There's a big square and there were other stores, because it was like a round circle that curved, where there was a sidewalk and it had all these different stores like Sears and CVS. And then, right in the middle, would be just this old, big place, the shelter, and then there were just beds. People could see in. They could break the glass. It was a small world and there was only about one little toy for kids. And then they couldn't cook, they couldn't eat, and they were bums, and they did drugs and stuff and there was more beds up here, more up here. I thought it was going to be really bad. I was never in a shelter before. When we came here, I was surprised. It didn't turn out to be like I thought it was. It wasn't like I thought. That's how I thought it was going to be. I didn't know why people came to shelters.

I wouldn't tell other kids anything about the shelter because I wouldn't want to be embarrassed. I'm embarrassed by being in a shelter. Because I used to take dancing at my school and there was this girl who was real stuck up on herself. She saw this pair of ear muffs and she said "Oh, I feel so bad for that kid, whose ever those are, probably on welfare." That's what got me mad. She said that in a mean kind of voice. That was in my school now. She doesn't know that my mother gets welfare. I never tell anybody! I'm embarrassed because everybody thinks welfare is stupid. They think everybody that's on welfare is just somebody that is a homo. I don't even know what a homo is but I hear them saying that all the time. I bet they think that, because they're always saying "Oh I feel so sorry for this kid" just because they're on welfare. When they say that I feel like punching them. Of course, I would get in trouble. And then I would go to the principal and then punch him because he's stupid, that's why. Because he's stupid! My teacher knows I'm on welfare. She knows that I live here at the shelter. She's supposed to know those things. I don't think she likes it too much because she's always, always, yelling at me. She yells at me more than other kids. She yells at me for nothing. She yells at me a lot just because I'm in a shelter! I just don't like her. I absolutely don't like her.

I had to stay back since I came here too. This is my second time staying back. School's easy for me, but in Florida I didn't finish the whole year when I was supposed to for the second grade. We left too soon. And I was going to start third grade in Florida, but then, I don't know what happened and I had to go to second grade. I had to go to the second grade twice in Florida and once here. I don't know why. We didn't go for the end of the year, because it was around the time we left.

When I came here I didn't think a shelter was nice, I thought a shelter was just a place where all these druggies were at. I didn't think it was too good. There's no druggies in this shelter. If there was, my mother wouldn't even be here. She wouldn't be here in this shelter with druggies. My little sister and brother like living here, at least some of it. My mom doesn't like it that much. I don't know why she doesn't like it because it's none of my business.

So what I'd really like is to be out of this shelter, be rich and have my friends. People end up living in shelters because I guess some can't pay their rents or I don't know. I guess they don't work. They don't do anything.

COMMENTARY

Ingrid and Tara tell two different stories about becoming homeless. Ingrid had lived all her life in the same general locality. For her family, homelessness was the end result of being poor for many years and finally reaching the point where they could no longer afford to stay in a house. Tara, on the other hand, had become homeless on the heels of a long-distance move that followed a violent argument and separation between her parents. But in spite of the differences in their stories, both Tara and Ingrid in their own way had to confront the fact that a homeless shelter was their only alternative. They had to struggle to imagine what the shelter would be like and come to terms with being one of "the homeless." Tara and Ingrid's stories are not atypical.

For most children, becoming homeless is a foreign and traumatic experience. While a small number have been homeless before, the majority have never been inside a shelter or met a homeless person, particularly a homeless child. The sense of confusion these children experience is heightened by the fact that becoming homeless can happen quickly, often in a matter of days or hours. The word comes or a decision is made that the family must move. Parents are overwhelmed by the loss of their home and scramble for alternative arrangements. Working their way through the social service system, they manage to locate a shelter. In the process they often have little time to prepare their children for the move out of their home and into a shelter.

When they first hear the news, these children try to make sense out of what is happening to them and to their families. For all of them, this event is a dramatic life change. They attempt to explain to themselves what it means to have "nowhere to live." They work at imagining what life will be like in a shelter, how long they will be there, and how they will get out. Most significantly, they struggle to confront society's perception of "the homeless" and integrate these perceptions into their initial response to the shelter.

The Meaning of Homelessness

Although they may be unable to articulate it, even toddlers have a sense that "home" is different from other places. Home may be distinguished by virtue of its familiar and consistent qualities, or by the sense of belonging felt there. In a shelter or motel, children as young as three or four years of age are aware that they are not living at home. Most are keenly aware that something out of the ordinary has happened to their families resulting in their having to move out of their home and come to stay in "this place." Nearly all of the children know that living in this way is different and out of the ordinary, and that it is only a temporary situation.

The children's sense of not being "at home" is evident in the words they use to refer to the shelter. In their conversations with each other and other adults, some children refer to the place in which they are living as "the shelter" or "the motel" or by its formal name, for example, "Sunrise House." Some refer to it simply as "this place." But even for those who have spent up to a year in a shelter, it is never referred to as "my home" or "my house," or even as "my home for now." A five-year-old girl who had been living in a shelter for six months stated quite emphatically: "I'm going to move to a house! This ain't a house. It's a big house that's like a building. But I'm going to live in a house. I'm not living in a house now" (Katie). Similarly, in her story, Ingrid made it clear that she considered the shelter and a house two very different things. She reported that her friend at school "asked me if I lived in a house or a shelter and I said 'a shelter.' "

How children understand the experience of losing one's home and living "in this place" clearly reflects their level of cognitive development. Consistent with the egocentric thinking characteristic of children under six years, very young children are only aware of their own family's experience. They think about becoming homeless as something that has happened only to them, and perhaps to a few other families whom they have met in the shelter. The vocabulary that society uses to describe their situation, such as homelessness, shelter, or the homeless, is not understood by preschool children.

School-aged children and adolescents, however, are keenly aware of homelessness as a more general condition that affects many families. They speak of the homeless as "people who have no home," of homelessness as "what happens when you lose your home," and of shelters as "places for people without a home." Both Ingrid and Tara in their stories indicated that their families are part of a larger group of families who do not have a place to live.

But whether or not they understand the meaning of the term homelessness in a general sense, and regardless of how they refer to it, nearly all children perceive the place where they are now living as the last alternative. They know that people come to live here because there is no other place to live. Children of all ages understand that the shelter is the last stop before living in the street. "And so we came to this place, 'cause there was nowhere else to go" is a theme that occurs repeatedly in the stories of these children. Tara stated it explicitly: "I didn't even know what a shelter was except all people who have no place to go, that's where they go!"

In most stories, one hears the lack of control that children felt over the events that brought them to the shelter. Finding themselves in a shelter has made children aware not only of their powerlessness, but also of the powerlessness of their parents. For many children, this event represents the initial and frightening realization that their parents are not all-powerful.

Finally, some express relief that there was a safe haven when they thought there was nothing else. In spite of Tara's anger at having to come to the shelter, her pictorial representation of the shelter had "Wellcome" [*sic*] written over the door.

Imagining Life in the Shelter

When they are told or overhear that they will have to live in a shelter or motel, children, quite naturally, attempt to envision what it will be like. Most of these children have had no previous experience in a shelter. They have neither lived in nor visited one. Very young children often literally think of it as a state of "nowhere" or "non-house." As Sean, age six, described it, "I thought I was moving to nowhere, that I can't move to no more houses." Older children rely on vicarious experience, most often what they have seen or heard in the media about shelters and homeless people. These images often lead children to envision the worst, and some describe very vivid memories of what they thought it would be like. Some children worry about the physical condition of the shelter and describe their fantasy most frequently as "one big room" that would be in bad physical condition, "that would look all messed up with cracks and crayons drawn on the wall." Many are convinced that it will be a horrible experience. Others worry about living with a large number of people, particularly strangers. Their exposure to the media has led them to believe that these people are mostly "bums and druggies," or "people who live out of bags and stuff and sleep on the streets." One girl recounted her anticipation in this way: "My mother told me we were going to come to the shelter. She told me in the daytime. I thought it was going to be like what I saw on TV—dirty, no lights, no food, no nothing. My mother said it was a nice place and I liked it when I came over here, I liked it. So when I came, it was much better than I thought" (Isabella). Like many children who expect the worst, this girl found the shelter to be not as bad as she had imagined.

A small number of children imagine that the shelter will be better than their current circumstances, particularly when they learn they are going to a motel or hotel. They have never been to a motel and are excited to have the opportunity to live in what they assume is significant luxury. "First I thought, 'Wow, we're going to live in a motel. Wow!' But when we came here, I didn't like it" (Sam). These children quite naturally are disappointed when they find themselves in motels and hotels that fall far short of luxury.

Arriving at the Shelter

Because it represents the loss of their home, the move to the shelter is remembered by nearly all children as a significant and, often, a painful event. Some children can recount the story of the events that led to their coming to the shelter in sharp detail, even months and years later. In these detailed accounts, the children describe themselves as active participants in the move. One child described how each family member helped out: "Mommy carried the boxes. And I take them little stuff. And I taked the plates. And my other brother took the dishes" (Maysa). While the story may not be entirely consistent with the parents' version of the events, it is logically coherent. These children tell the story often to other children in the shelter, and to staff.

By contrast, other children do not clearly recall what transpired when they moved. The confusing series of events that led to such an abrupt and drastic change in their lives blurs their perception of what has taken place. These children are unclear about many of the details of getting to the shelter and often describe a sequence of events that happens almost without their participation. A young adolescent boy who came from Puerto Rico and immediately went to a shelter described the events as follows:

> So we didn't have a place to go but I was sleeping. I didn't know we got to the police department. I was sleeping. The taxi man took us here to the shelter by taxi, too. I don't remember being in the police department. I was sleeping in the back of the car. I stayed in the taxi and my mom just went in the police department. It was in the middle of the night, like three or two in the morning. I just kept sleeping. We had no place to go and the police said go here. It's for people that has no place to go. (Jose)

In these stories of arrival at the shelter, children do not mask their feelings about having to come to this place. Some are disappointed. Many are angry. Tara's anger is clearly heard in her story and is directed every-where, at the bus passengers, at the shelter staff and guests, at her teacher, and her friends. With an intense anger, she declared in many different ways what she finally stated unequivocally: "I hate this place."

Feeling Ashamed

Whether their original expectations leave them disappointed or surprised, these children are all aware that having to come to a shelter is a humiliating and degrading experience. Young children are less likely to state this directly, but instead describe the potential of other children making fun of them. "They'll all laugh at me because I live in the shelter" was heard in story after story.

As they begin to develop their sense of identity, children tend to compare themselves to their peers. School-aged homeless children are able to note a crucial difference between themselves and their peers. They realize that they are without the home that other children have, and they feel ashamed and rejected. In the words of one nine-year-old girl: "If my friends knew I was here, they wouldn't like it. They'll go with other friends. Because they've never been through something like this, I don't think they'd like me. Maybe they've never gone through this problem before" (Isabella).

As they move toward adolescence, children become more articulate about how degraded they feel. "It's pretty poor, pretty low living in a shelter. I hate it." This comment captures the loss of dignity felt by one young adolescent. Older children are often aware of the various connotations that homelessness has. To them, the shame comes not only from not having a home, but from being classified as "the shelter people."

For all of these children, becoming a shelter person has to a greater or lesser degree resulted in a change in their definition of themselves. Homelessness has made clear and concrete to them the fact that they are homeless because they do not have enough money, that in fact, they are very poor. A major contributor to the shame of homelessness for these children lies in the fact of their poverty. They see themselves as "have-nots," as the people for whom other people feel sorry. One fourteen-year-old girl described how other kids reacted to her and her friends from the shelter, referring to them as shelter people. She said: "They think 'shelter people' are poor! Poor like they can't get a house or something. Bums and stuff. They probably think people who live in shelters sit around the house all day . . ." (April).

These perceptions are confirmed for many homeless children by the numerous public collections for the homeless. Particularly during the Thanksgiving and Christmas seasons, children are sensitive to the media campaigns soliciting money and other items for the homeless. Ironically, many of these children participate in such collections for the homeless and poor in school. In a phenomenon that seems like the recycling of poverty, these children often ask shelter staff for permission to take cans of food for the school collection from the shelter pantry, which has just received this food as a donation. These public solicitations serve to remind children of their painful situation. Ingrid described this experience in her school, saying: "When they start collecting food for the poor in school, sometimes I feel like I'm poor. I feel bad about it. It makes me feel sad."

Further, and most significantly for the children's self-concept, poverty represents not simply deprivation of money and material goods but a judgment on their worth as people. They sense clearly society's judgment of poverty as a morally inferior status. These children feel they are inferior, even bad because of their poverty. The judgment that they are poor is also a judgment that they are unworthy. For all these reasons, children feel sad, vulnerable, and ultimately ashamed because they are poor. It is society's judgment about the poor that they ultimately integrate into their definition of themselves. The "bad" of being poor becomes part of their definition of who they are.

Identifying with Stereotypes of the Homeless

Another aspect of their shame arises from what they perceive to be society's perception of homeless people. They know that homeless people are perceived in a generally negative way by society and they are quite articulate about the familiar images of poverty. Prior to coming to the shelter, they had a detailed set of impressions about what kind of people are in shelters and who the homeless are. Nearly all of them had the image of homeless people that is presented most often in the media, the "bag ladies" who raid rubbish barrels, or the alcoholic men who sleep on the sidewalks and park benches, or "druggies and bums." An eight-year-old girl vividly remembered her expectations:

Before I came here like, when my mother mentioned the shelter, I thought she meant the kind in Boston which has rats and one big room. I read about it in the newspaper and I saw them on TV. I saw all these people on TV who were, like, I don't know. You know what shelter means to me? It means like people who are bums and stuff. But no one here are bums. Everyone's the opposite of bums. On TV I saw people who lived on bags and stuff. And I used to live out of a suitcase when we were in the motel before this shelter. But now I'm going to live out of a bureau. Anyway, I said, "Mom, I don't want to go to a shelter." And she said, "Maybe, maybe not." She didn't know like whether we'd be going and like we're lucky we got this kind of a shelter 'cause they have things for children and they're nice people who work here. And they play with us and they spray for roaches too. (Vicky)

A high school senior who was in the shelter with his mother and five younger siblings had similar perceptions about being homeless: "When I think of a shelter, I think like a big room with cots and things, not something like this. The word 'shelter,' I thought of the shelters up in the city, for all the people on the streets and stuff. My mother said it wasn't like that" (T. J.).

The identification of "bums and druggies" in the shelter is not only threatening to their sense of personal safety, but also embarrassing in terms of their being identified with these groups whom they perceive to be social outcasts. They struggle to integrate these initial images with the images they have gained of other families and children in the shelter, as well as with what they know about themselves and their families, families that are "poor but nice people." While they are quick to describe their family as different from "the bag ladies or street bums," they make the distinction with more or less conviction in their voice and words depending upon their particular circumstances. This is particularly the case for children who are aware of substance abuse in their families or in other families in the shelter. This group of children is quite aware that somehow the drugs and alcohol are related to their being homeless. Even children who do not have substance abuse in their family think that other children assume they do. They often feel guilty by association.

Children respond to these feelings by trying to differentiate themselves and their families from the typical perception of "druggies and bums." Eleven-year-old Troy struggled to make the distinction:

If kids found out I lived in a shelter they would laugh at me because some of them have houses and some of them have apartments. None of them is living in a shelter. Because they're all rich and have a place to live and they're rich and stuff. I'm living with somebody else. I'm living in a shelter and my mother's homeless so that means I'm a homeless children. . . . If kids knew I lived in a shelter, they'd start calling me "homeless." I don't know what they'd say. I bet they think homeless people are bums, alkies, druggies. I don't think that's true. Homeless people are just homeless. They're homeless because they don't have enough money.

A nine-year-old child, whose mother had difficulty managing what little money she had, differentiated himself from the homeless:

> They're always talking about the homeless and everything. They'll talk about the homeless and shelters and call the kids in the shelter "homeless." I'm not homeless right now cause this place makes me feel like I have a home. "Homeless," I think, is people out on the streets. Those people should just go do something about it. Like they should go to a place like this. They could go to the day centers; they're like a home. They're there until night. But people on the streets don't like to go to a shelter. I don't think people like to go there unless they're junkies. (Tucker)

Moving Again

For many of these children, becoming homeless not only means dealing with the perceptions of homeless people that others have, it also means living through a major move. For a sizeable number of children, the shelter or motel is only the latest in a long list of addresses. The repeated moving presents as much of a problem to some of these children as the living in a shelter or motel. Some children can recount in sequence the street addresses or cities or states in which they have lived. They often use their school history to jog their memories. Statements such as "when I was in first grade, I was in Florida. And then I went to Arkansas for the beginning of second and then to Florida again" are not uncommon. Many, particularly the younger children, report that they move so much because their parents say they should or because their parents no longer like where they are currently living and say "we're going to move." One four-year-old insisted: "I wanna have a house. I wanna live there. I don't wanna move any more. Mommy said we had to move" (Mario).

As they get older, children can explain more clearly why they resent the frequent moving. Their resentment is motivated largely by issues of peer relationships, which have developed prominent roles in their lives. They are repeatedly losing old friends and trying to make new ones.

Despite their ability to articulate reasons why they should not move, these children perceive that they are relatively powerless to change their transient lifestyle. Ten-year-old Stephanie, who has moved around the country about fifteen times in her life, described her frustration:

> We had to leave when it snowed. My parents said so. We moved because we were going to Texas. We have to move so much because some spots we don't like and some spots we like. My mother and my father decide to move and then we tell them what, what we want.

She continued: "Sometimes I get mad that we have to move so much. I tell dad or my mom. They say 'We won't move but we have to move sometimes.' Then we move a lot of times."

Envisioning Leaving the Shelter

Consistent with their immature level of cognitive development, many of the preschool-aged children are quite vague about how long they have been in the shelter and how long they will have to remain. Some mention a specific period of time that they have heard adults quote, for example, ninety days, but have little concrete idea what that means. Five-year-old Doreen explained: "We're living here now but we're not going to stay here, not all the time. We're going to get another place but I don't know when that's going to happen." Another five-year-old girl reported that "we moved a lot of times, like fifty times. I lived in a motel for fifty years. No, like sixty years" (Gertie).

School-age children tend to use concrete markers to indicate the time, such as, "we came here just before school started," and begin to be aware of the open-ended nature of their stay. They slowly realize that neither they nor their parents have any control over the length of stay, which they perceive as decided by "official" people.

Adolescents are very conscious of the unpredictability of their length of stay. Additionally, they are very aware of the discrepancy between the official word and how long some of the present residents already have been there. They know that promises about when the certificate will come or housing will be available will often not be kept.

While most children realize that they are waiting to get their own house, they vary in terms of how specifically they understand how this is going to be accomplished. Younger children are much vaguer about how they will actually obtain a house. Eight-year-old Paul stated: "We're going to be here for a little while, for about two months. We're waiting for something but I don't really know what we're waiting for."

On the other hand, most older children seem to have a clearer grasp of how they are going to get out of the shelter and what the bureaucratic process will be. While he does not specifically articulate the catch-22 dimension of the process of finding a permanent place to live, this twelve-year-old boy's description indicates that he has experienced it. He, like many of these children, felt trapped by the rules of the system:

People have to come to a shelter to get an apartment, Section 8, to get an apartment you don't have to pay for. You don't have to get your money, Section 8 pays for it. People need Section 8 maybe that can't have a job. To just get Section 8 they have to come to the shelter. We can't get an apartment if we don't get Section 8 because we just, we didn't have no money because my mom she cannot work because she's taking coupons for the food. So she can't have a job. She needs money for the apartment. It's because she just doesn't have the money. Some people have money 'cause they work, maybe they work. If my mom worked, we'd still have to come to the shelter, because we have to get an apartment and live for right now. You have to have money first to get an apartment. And we gotta get a home and just move out. The rest of the people are here in the shelter to get a brand new home and some people just stay for a Section 8 and they get it and get a home. (Jose)

Depending on their age, children have varying levels of understanding about how long they will be in the shelter and how the process by which they will get out works. Similarly, they also have different types of understanding about where the shelter is located with respect to their old home. In an attempt to get geographically oriented, many children try to figure out where the shelter is, particularly with respect to their "house." The location of the shelter is often a mystery to children, particularly younger children for whom the concept of distance is not well developed. Younger children tend to locate themselves by using various concrete indicators of distance, such as the length of time on the bus, or the distance on the map. One seven-year-old boy who had moved from the Deep South to the Northeast used his arms and his memory of the map to locate the distance between "my house and this place." Pointing down to his feet with one hand and stretching up over his head with the other, he said: "We came from way down here in the purple on the map to way up here to the green on the map. We're right on the curvy thing on the map. The green is very far away from the purple." Older children are quite aware of the distances involved, and in particular how it impacts their being able to see the friends or family members they had to leave behind.

In coming to the shelter, children are trying to get their bearings. They are dealing with their fears about what the shelter will be like and about who will be living there. They are confronting society's perceptions of the homeless, and are trying to sort out how long they will be there and how they will get out. The most difficult aspect of becoming homeless, however, seems to be the radical shift in children's identity. Becoming homeless represents a judgment on their worth as people. When Troy said of himself "now I'm a homeless children," he did so with all the surplus meaning that homelessness has in our society.

Chapter Three

"Because We're Poor":
Explanations of Homelessness

SEAN

Sean, age six, and his brother Marcus, age eight, have been living in the shelter with their mother and three-year-old sister for over two months. They left a large East Coast city and came to live with the maternal grandmother in this current city. The move to the shelter was precipitated by a fight between the mother and the grandmother, the latter urging her daughter to learn to "stand on her own two feet." Their father separated from their mother several years ago and lives out of state.

My brother is Marcus and I'm Sean and I'm 6. I go to school to first grade. I just finished. I go to East Side School. I go on a bus. I know how to read pretty good. I can read about a frog. I saw a frog the other night. And guess what I did? I ran away. I don't like frogs. We can go outside around the house when we play. We go in the parking lot. My other friend across the street plays baseball. We been living here maybe a month. I like the beds. The best thing is I can watch TV. The worst thing is you can't watch TV early. Like until nine o'clock in the morning, because they won't let you put the TV on. Sometimes, on the weekends they let you watch the TV.

Before we were living here I was living beside my grandmother's house. It was in Elliot. We lived there for a long time. We had to move to this house because my mother didn't have enough money to pay the bills. The man that owned the house he said if you don't got enough money to pay your bills then you have to go somewhere else. And my mommy said "Okay," so then we move. I didn't know where we were going. Maybe we go to another house but we didn't go to another house. Then we came here. I think it was great, sort of. I don't like kids bothering me. . . . The other kids bother me sometimes. But if they bother me, I walk away from them. I don't get in trouble. But one time I got in trouble. One of these little kids said "He hit me," when I didn't. He said I hit him but I didn't. Doug got me in trouble. He blamed me.

Where I used to live, before here, sometimes Mommy didn't have enough money and I'd get worried a little bit. I was worried that I thought I was moving to nowhere—that I can't move to no more houses. Then I thought I was going to a big, big house. With a lot of people. No, not a lot of people, but people in apartments. When I came here, I thought it was nice. My mother has her own room. I sleep with my brother, but we each have our own beds. I sleep in my own bed. My mother has to share with my sister. She's three years old. I have a lot of cousins. Sometimes I see my Dad. He moved. I haven't seen him since I came here. I wish I could see him. Sometimes I get sad. I like him. He's tall! I'm tall too, the tallest kid in the first grade. There are two kids that are bigger than me.

When I grow up, I'm going to be a church preacher. We go to the church by my grandma's. It's my grandma's church. I go only on Sundays. I like the preacher there. When I'm a church preacher, I'd like to say that I like everybody.

When we had to move my grandma said I could come and live with her and my mother said no. Because before I was living with her and I moved from the other apartment too. My mother can't pay the bills because she doesn't have enough money. I don't know why. She used to get her money from a bank. I don't know where she gets it now. Sometimes she gets if from the bank, but I don't know where she gets her other money. We had enough food but my mom didn't have enough money to pay for the house. We didn't have no money for a car either.

The kids at school don't know that we moved over here. My teacher didn't tell them. I don't want my teacher to tell them. If kids knew I lived here, they'd laugh. They think it's funny because they're not living in a shelter, that's why they'd think it's so funny. A shelter's for people who don't got apartments. Only one thing I know about living here is that J. J. had to move here and I know why. He had a fire. He had a fire in his house. And that's why he had to move because they didn't have any place.

I moved here first then he moved here after I moved here. He ask me why I'm living here and I said that we didn't have enough money for the bills from my house. J. J. saved up some money and he gave it to me. But he didn't make that much. It wasn't enough money. We need a lot of money.

We might move next week. We found an apartment. I saw it. It's a big house. It's a new, green house. I like it. It's got rooms inside of it. It's got good floors and it's got good rugs. I forgot the street. All our furniture from our other house, Mommy couldn't take it because she can't go back in the house. It's all gone. We're going to get furniture from the store. There's already furniture in the house, but all we need is one little couch. And we need a rocking chair because my mom might want to rock in a chair. It's got beds. From my old house, I got my clothes and my toys but they're not over here. They're at my auntie's house. But not my furniture. My mother couldn't get back in the house. I'm getting new furniture in my apartment.

Next year, after we move, I'm not going to the same school. I'm going maybe to Michael's school. Maybe like a church school. I like going to church. Sometimes I pray. I ask God about the house. I ask God to help me find a house. I say "I hope I find a nice house God." God says "You'll find one."

My mommy don't think it's good to be living in a shelter because she don't like it. Because people kept getting into fights and sometimes she gets into them too. Fights in the shelter. She doesn't like it. There is one thing she don't like about the shelter. She don't like fighting. My mommy gave me my haircut. I like it. Some people say I look like I'm nine years old and I'm only six.

IAN

Ian, who is fifteen, and his family have a history of unstable living situations. He and his mother have been in shelters on five previous occasions. Before coming to the current shelter, they were living in a hotel. Ian has also spent time in a residential school for troubled youths. During this shelter stay, he and his mother are joined by his one-year-old brother, David. Ian's father abandoned his mother prior to his birth. The mother was recently separated from his stepfather of many years.

I'm fifteen and I go to Osgood High. I'm a freshman. I'm going to be a sophomore. We're getting out for the summer on Monday. Getting out is awesome. I hate school. I hate Osgood High. See my hair? It's spiked and I dyed it blond. All Osgood High is filled with jocks. I don't like jocks. They rank on me all the time. Because I skateboard and they don't like my hair. It's not natural. This isn't a natural style. It's punk. They don't like it. To be a jock you have to have long hair and nice, neat hair. It can't look different or anything. There's some kids there like me, like four of them. Those are my friends. We go to the city square and skate all the time and stuff. We hang out over there. That's the only place we're really wanted. . . .

We came here about December, the end of December. Now it's the end of June. We didn't have anywhere to live. We lived at my grandfather's, but my grandparents don't get along with my mother, so they kicked her out. So we came here. We were living with them about two or three years. My grandparents are rich. Wicked rich. They're low. They're wicked low. We're living in a shelter and my mother's mother and father are so rich. I hate them. I didn't like them even when we were there. Not really. They're not normal. They're crazy. They treat my mother like crap all the time. There was five of them, mother's two brothers live there, and they're like twenty-four and twenty-eight and like if they make a mess my mother has to clean it up. Even if my uncle makes a mess, and he doesn't clean it up, my mother gets screamed at for it. Because when they were little my mother took care of the whole family because my grandmother and my grandfather were out making money. So, my mother quit school in ninth grade. She was the oldest one. She quit to take care of the kids. But now my grandmother doesn't understand that they're all adults and they all can take care of themselves. My mom can't do everything for everybody all the time. My mother wants respect and she told them and they got mad and so we had to get out. They get mad at my mother for not having her own place.

My grandmother wouldn't come to the shelter for my birthday. I don't know why. My friends won't visit me here either. They think it's a bum shelter. Bums! I wouldn't live with bums. I wouldn't let my mother or my brother live with bums either. I'd rob somebody before I'd live with bums. Some of my friends think it's pretty bad, but not all of them. Most of them understand. But some, they're not really my friends but I see them sometimes, they don't understand. I don't want anybody to know that I live here. They know because I told my other friends that live in the projects, my kind of friends, but I don't hang around with those other kids. Like one day I was skating with my friends and those other friends are with my friends and they just found out where I live. They didn't say nothing though. One time, one of my friends talked, like joking around, and I didn't like it. He said, "Oh, I'm going to go take a shower in the shelter." And I almost beat the crap out of him. I took a fit and started screaming and pushing. He told me to come on and I hit him in the head. And then he goes "I was just joking." Because he was in a school like I used to be in, so I made fun of that too, so he says, "you made fun of that school." So that's why he said about the shelter and stuff. . . .

I don't know why we ended up here and not in another apartment. Somehow my mother went on welfare and she can't get her certificate for an apartment. So she's waiting. She wouldn't have enough money to do it on her own. And my stepfather can't do it because he's paying all the car payments. My grandfather won't lend my mother any money either. He lends everybody else a lot of money to get nice houses and stuff, but he can't lend my mother the money to get a three-bedroom apartment. My grandmother treats my mother bad. I don't know, I think she used to abuse my mother or something. I think. I'm not sure. I think so though. Because my Uncle Joe told me when they were little that it happened. When my mother was pregnant with me, my grandfather punched her because my grandmother didn't want her to be pregnant because she wasn't married. They're wicked Catholic. I don't believe in God because it's so dumb. Sitting there praying to a wall. He doesn't do nothing back. It's just dumb. I don't like God. I just don't like him. I hate going to church. It's boring. You have to sit and listen to a priest say stuff you don't even know about. It doesn't make sense. You don't learn nothing. I don't learn nothing from going to church. I haven't been to church in three years. I don't like God. There is no God. He's not even there.

Living here is not that bad. My mother met a good friend, she made a good friend here. They're best friends right now. She's best friends with her. Her friend does a lot for us and we do a lot for her. Like chores and stuff. . . .

There's nothing good about living here, I just have to. We'll probably be here about five more months. We can't get out sooner because welfare stinks. And for housing you can't get the certificate. We're just waiting. There's three-bedroom apartments that we need. They're in the projects right now, but don't ask me why we can't have it. I don't understand it. I don't understand how they work. I know about the three-bedroom apartments because of my friends live in the projects and there's nobody living in those apartments. Two apartments have three bedrooms. And they're painted and cleaned out and everything. They're nice. I don't really want to go to the projects. One project is okay, but definitely not the other one. It has gang fights, knife fights, all different gangs. It's like, if you're not Black or Puerto Rican you'll get killed. . . .

Before we came to live here, my mother told me we were coming to a shelter. I was mad. I had no idea what I was going to get into. I was mad because a shelter is bad. It's pretty poor, pretty low living in a shelter. I hate it. It's pretty low because it's like you can't afford to live anywhere else. We could afford it but we just can't find a place and stuff.

The rest of the people are here because they're poor. They're poor just like anybody else. Or their houses burned down or something. I don't really talk to them that much. I talk to some of them. I ignore everybody when they talk on the phone. I don't talk to them about living here. Before I came, I thought it was going to be like a house where we just had our own room, except my mother and my brother would share one room and I had my own room. It was like different apartments in a house, like a hotel. I thought it was going to be like that. And I found out we got only one room, and I got pretty mad again. I was mad because of one room. It's better having your own room. Privacy's better. You can't just share a room with your mother and your brother. I was real mad. I didn't know what to do. I didn't want to get mad, but you get mad about certain things, like when someone takes something away from you. You know how to get mad about that. I didn't know how to get mad about this because this has never happened before. I don't know. I was mad at my mom and stuff for not working and not putting David into daycare. She said she won't. She said that's why I took fits, because she wasn't around me enough. She's messed up. I don't know. I think she's messed up, but just like any other mom. She was twenty-one when I was born. I'm fifteen now. . . .

The worst part of living in a shelter is just not having an apartment, not having your own house to live in. Having to live in a shelter, that's the worst part.

I'm still mad at my mom, but not really. I don't care. I don't even know if we're going to be out of here when I go back to school. I don't know. For the summer, I'm going to have fun—just not to go to school. I hate school so bad. I just made it this year. I had forty absences all year. I was absent so much because we were moving around so much. I missed a lot of days of school because we were moving around so much, from my grandmother's house to a hotel and then to the shelter. No, my grandmother's house to my mother's friend's house, then to my other mother's friend's house, then back to my mother's friend's house, then to the hotel and then to the shelter.

We walked in the hotel at night. It was pretty good. It was nice. It was the Court Motor Inn. That's the place that we went first after we left my mother's friend's. A friend of mine knew it was nice. But still not as good as having an apartment. I don't know if it's better than living here at the shelter. It's hard to decide. Neither of them are terrific. The hardest part about the hotel was the same thing as here, because you only have one room. The people here are better because there's people here my mother met. We have good friends. She met people at the hotel, but they're just there for a little while and then they don't live around here. It's a hotel, and they don't live there very long. They're all not there because they're poor. They stay for a while, like three or four days a week. They just happen to be staying there. I think one other family was there because they were poor and that's it. I'm not sure. We were at the hotel a month or two. I'd say a month. And then, we were on a waiting list to get in here. I think things are going to get better when I get out of here. They definitely will. It's going to be awesome, having your own apartment and stuff and having your own room. I can bring friends over and stuff. Having my own room, I can put posters all over the walls and stuff. I can have a TV and VCR. . . .

I don't like this town. I always lived here but I don't like it. I didn't live here for a while. I got kicked out of elementary school and I was in this private school at St. Mary's in Wilton. I was there, I lived there for a year and a half. I was at the state hospital, too, for mental kids, but I didn't deserve to be there because it's like for juveniles, not like, for kids with problems like me. I was only there for a little while, because they didn't know where to put me, because there weren't any openings anyplace else. I was in fifth grade then. The other place I was at, St. Mary's, was a school. I lived there. It was alright. It's a good school. I didn't like living there because you can't do nothing there. They treat you like eight-year-olds. Then I came back to this town for high school. I was at St. Mary's for sixth, seventh, and eighth grade. Before the state hospital place, I was living with my mother. I wanted to go back home. I had no feelings at that school I stayed at. Shit, I lived with this goober. This geek. He's a goob. He's weird. I don't know, just weird. He'd just throw stuff around and stuff. He'd get mad so easy and you wouldn't even know it. He could flip out right away, start swinging. They helped you with your mad stuff there. I'm doing better with that now. I haven't tooken a fit in so long, just little ones. . . .

One of my uncles is still doing cocaine but he doesn't do it around me because I'm old enough. He'll know I'll throw him out. I'd do something. And if he does it around my brother he knows I'll kick the crap out of him. I'll punch him in the head. When I was a kid, I knew cocaine was drugs, but I didn't know what it was like, what kind. I knew it was bad.

I'm never going to do it. I would never try cocaine, never, because it kills you so fast. It's the worst drug. I'd be so scared to take it. I wouldn't do acid either. But pot's nothing. Some people say it can lead to addiction but not to me. I don't do pot. I try not to. I do it sometimes though. I would never do coke. Pot, it would never lead me to coke, that's nuts. I'm not a druggie. I'd never do nothing with a needle, never. I would never do it. I used to smoke, but I quit last year. That's why I'm so small. I'm fifteen. I started smoking when I was nine, from nine to fourteen I smoked. That's why I'm so small. Look how small I am. That might be the reason, you never know. Hopefully I'll shoot up. The jocks are about three feet bigger than me. If I was their size, I'd fight them all. But I'm not. They'd kill me. I used to smoke a lot, no maybe normal, just like everybody else. A pack a day, maybe. When I was nine I didn't smoke hardly at all, but then like at thirteen and fourteen, I smoked about a pack a day. I'm small but I'm fast. My friends said I have strong legs. I have strong knees, it doesn't look like it, but I do. I only play baseball. I would never play a sport at school. I don't want to. I don't like jocks. I'm prejudiced against jocks. Because they go around school thinking they're big and bad, like they own school. I know it doesn't make a lot of difference if you're small but, to them it does. I'm fast. I can handle myself. My best friend is Bruce. He plays football but he's not a jock. He's such a good kid. I've known him since a year before kindergarten. I like him. But I don't hang around with him that much, because he doesn't skate. I have other friends I can talk to when I'm upset about something. I talk with anybody really. Any of my friends. Sometimes when I get upset, I can talk to my mother. Sometimes. But that's hard because some things you just don't talk to your mother about. My stepfather, too, he's not the kind that talks. He's not the kind of type that goes out with a lot of girls. He's short and skinny. I used to have a girl. She went to Montana. I got a picture of her. She's sixteen now, she was fifteen in this picture and I was fourteen. . . .

And I hate this shelter. The only good thing we'll get out of it is an apartment. So it's worth it. We have to do it. There's no choice.

COMMENTARY

In their attempts to make meaning out of the experience of becoming homeless, Sean and Ian both struggle with the question of why they have lost their homes. Sean's explanation is concrete and simple: his mother didn't have enough money to pay the bills. Ian, who is significantly older, offers a more complex explanation. He presents multiple, interrelated reasons for why his family eventually became homeless. He is aware that homelessness ultimately reflects larger problems and issues: family dysfunction, substance abuse, social welfare services, and housing policies. Sean and Ian continually reflect, as all children do, on the reasons for their homelessness.

A major part of children's stories of homelessness is the explanation they give to themselves and to others about how they lost their home. What are the reasons that homelessness happened to their family, in particular, and to other families more generally? How do the children make meaning out of what has happened to them? What is the story children tell themselves, not only about what is happening, but most critically, about why it is happening? Children have many stories about the causes of their homelessness. While all children are generally aware that they are living in a shelter because they lost their home, children differ from one another in terms of how they explain why that has happened to their family. Their understanding of why they came to be homeless or had to live in a shelter is quite clearly related to their level of cognitive development.

Preschoolers' Explanations

Preschool-aged children, whose thinking processes are not yet logical, are unable to reason in terms of cause and effect. While they may report a cause for particular events in their lives, they are unable to explain how the cause produced the event. They explain the connection between events in terms of associations. Instead of being able to describe how a specific event produced their homelessness, they present only a disjointed account of some events that are associated with, but not necessarily the primary cause of, their homelessness. Consequently, they present a fairly confused and disconnected account of why they had to move out of their home. They have bits and pieces of a story that do not form a cohesive explanation. In accounting for why they lost their home, some young children may describe an incident as causing their becoming homeless, although from an adult's perspective, the incident only happened to coincide with, but did not cause, the event.

For example, a six-year-old boy, whose family had lived in many shelters, described the first time they lost their home, when he was four years old, and moved into the Salvation Army shelter. He attributed the loss of the home to the appearance of new tenants on the doorstep:

Once we were living in our place and some people came up the front stairs with all their stuff like brooms and suitcases and stuff. And when they got up the stairs they was moving in. So we had to get out by the back door. They was moving in the front door. They needed a place to live. They came to where we was living and we had no place to go. So we went to the Sally. (Bobby)

Another child, who was five years old, attributed her coming to the shelter to the stove in their old house. Explained Doreen:

We lived in Chicago. Why I came to here is because we had another one and then we moved out of there. And then we moved out of the other one and then we moved here. We moved out of the other one because in the other one, the stove, my mother was burning the whole house maybe. It was the stove. So we had to move here.

Rather than a specific incident, a feeling associated with the move, such as a like or dislike, may be viewed by some young children as the event that caused the loss of home. Many young children, for example, attribute their moving from their old home to the preference of the parent rather than the necessity of circumstances. Referring to his old house, Daniel, a four-year-old, insisted they had moved "because I didn't like it and Mommy and Daddy didn't like it either." Arthur, a five-year-old who had moved with his mother and three younger sisters from the South to the North, attributed their leaving their home to the mother's preference for living in a pretty place. "Momma say to come here because she want us to come here. Because she liked it here. Because it's pretty." Arthur's mother, on the other hand, reported that she moved away from an abusive husband and came north for better job opportunities.

While some young children propose only a single cause, others list multiple causes. They simply list these causes as separate events and do not explain any connections between these causes. A seven-year-old girl, for example, provided several reasons for the move, each of which were associated with the family's moving out of the apartment. However, the reasons are not linked together in a logical manner and are disjointed and confusing:

We're not living in our house now because when we used to live there the owner went away for twenty days and after twenty days he came back and he told us to get out. I got lead poison there. It's like when I was a baby I drank paint and I got sick. . . . So I got lead poisoning there so the guy that owned the house came back. And a girl said "Get out." My mom and my dad said, "You can't do that.

We lived here, then you moved out, so you can't come back in here. Too bad." Me and my mom owned that house. Me and my dad and my mom and my two brothers. Me and my brothers put some of our money in. We had two hundred bucks and put some of our money in and my mom and my dad put some of their money in. Everybody in our family, but me and my sister, they put some money in. (Gertie)

Because children at this age cannot reason in a logical fashion—that is, they do not understand that causes produce necessary effects—they do not see the world as a predictable place. Things happen randomly and chaotically. The positive aspect of this way of thinking is that it provides children with the ability to view the world in a hopeful way. Anything can happen "by magic." For example, they can believe that they will "have a house next week" without thinking about how that is going to happen. On the other hand, children's perception of events as random and magical occurrences does not foster a sense of control over the events around them. If events unfold spontaneously with no cause or necessary effect, then children are powerless to regulate any of the happenings in their lives. They are simply victims of whatever the environment does to them. It is this sense of lack of control that pervades young children's stories of how they became homeless.

While young children have varied explanations for the causes of their homelessness, surprisingly few, if any, attribute the homelessness to something that they did or failed to do. By contrast, in other traumatic situations, for example being placed in foster care or losing a parent to death, young children are very likely to report that they are personally responsible. The egocentric thinking characteristic of this stage of cognitive development leads them to believe that their actions have more effect than is actually possible. Consequently, they are inclined to believe that they are the cause of bad events. For example, an eight-year-old who had been placed in foster care when she was five clung to her early beliefs and explained that "we went into foster care because my brother and me didn't keep our room neat, it was a mess. The social work lady went all over our house and took us. The social workers are the bad people. They're off us now so we can keep our room how we want" (Jamie).

By contrast, young children who lose their homes do not seem to blame themselves as individuals for becoming homeless. It seems that children perceive their role in family separations quite differently from their role in the loss of their home. At the core of family separations are interpersonal relationships, in which children are active participants.

Children learn from an early age that in these relationships they have
certain power. For example, a child learns the connection "I smile, they
smile." Thus, if these relationships go bad, children find it easy to believe
that they played a significant role. Becoming homeless appears to be
viewed as an issue of household management, an aspect of life in which
children play no role. Getting money, paying bills, finding an apartment,
and the like are "the stuff mommies and daddies do." These household
management tasks are taken care of externally, and they are foreign to
children. Thus, young children may perceive themselves as powerless to
control these events. It may be that in this way children are spared from
attributing the loss of their home to themselves.

School-aged Children's Explanations

In contrast to younger children, school-aged children between the ages
of approximately seven and twelve do provide logically coherent explanations for their becoming homeless. Their explanations are likely to
involve one or a few concrete events that they perceive as directly
resulting in their homelessness, such as "the ceiling fell in," "we ran out
of money," "boys hung around our house," or "Mom said to move."
Unlike the case with younger children, these events are not merely
associated with homelessness. Children at this age can provide some
explanation for how each of these events led to homelessness. Some
children focus on a single reason for their becoming homeless, such as
"the owner kicked us out," while others offer multiple reasons for the
family's becoming homeless.

Often children at this age offer a list of reasons. For example, after
describing how her family had made many moves into "better apartments" within the city in order to get away from "bad apartments" in
drug-infested areas, ten-year-old Isabella explained:

> The last apartment was perfect, at first. But then the rain came in
> the spring and the ceiling got wet and fell down. And that's how we
> found out it had lead in the paint. That's bad. There was roaches
> too. I would kill them every time I see them. So my mother came
> here to the shelter to see if we could get in.

Isabella further explained that their homelessness also resulted from an
inability to pay for another apartment, the presence of drugs in their
previous neighborhoods, small apartments being inadequate for her
family's size, and a landlord who was "very bad," having "lied to us

about the lead paint." Isabella clearly attributed her homelessness to multiple causes.

While children in this stage can explain how each separate event or condition in and of itself led to homelessness, they are not usually able to explain how all these events are interconnected. Isabella could provide a string of causes and the specific effect of each, yet she was unable to articulate how these multiple causes were interrelated, for example, that lack of money made it difficult to get a good-sized, clean apartment in a safe neighborhood.

At this stage, the causes children offer are still concrete, but they are less individualistic and somewhat more general than those of younger children. For example, while a five-year-old might suggest that they are homeless "because my aunt Lisa kicked us out," school-aged children explain that "you can't stay with relatives because the landlord says there's too many people in the apartment." Children at this stage are also able to distinguish between different types of reasons, for example, momentary and more enduring causes. Tucker reported:

> We came to the shelter because we moved up to our other grandmother's and they kicked us out! Well, our other grandmother didn't kind of kick us out, she just said "You gotta learn how to stay on your own. Your mother has to learn how to stay on her own, stand on her own feet, because soon I'm going to die and I'm not going to be there to help her." So that's why we came to the shelter.

Tucker realized that, while the immediate cause was his grandmother's order to get out, the more enduring cause was his mother's inability to manage on her own.

As a further extension of the ability to think in more general and less egocentric terms, children at this age are likely to recognize fundamental causes of homelessness rather than a series of discrete or distinct causes. For example, while school-aged children give many and diverse reasons for becoming homeless, nearly all include lack of money as one of those reasons. These children are quite aware that homelessness is a condition that affects not only their family, but many families, and that one cause for almost every family's homelessness is not having enough money to pay for a house.

Another, more general cause recognized by children this age is a "bad neighborhood," where there are a lot of problems, for example, drugs, violence, or substandard housing. They are beginning to recognize that there are better and worse places to live, and that they were living in the latter. While they cannot articulate the precise connection, they are aware that problems in finding a safe and adequate place to live are somehow related to their being homeless. A ten-year-old recalled:

> First we lived on Westwood and then Main and then Central. We moved from Westwood because there was a lot of bad things in Westwood—a lot of drugs and bad things. And my mother then moved to Main and she had to move from Main because it was too stretchy, it was too little, the apartment, all our furniture wouldn't fit and from Main she moved to Central and Central was perfect, but one day the ceiling fell off on my house. (Isabella)

In a similar manner, children at this age also begin to recognize that the rules of the larger system play some role in their becoming homeless and in their ability to get another house. While they cannot explain all the pieces in a cohesive manner, some do understand that being homeless will actually help them to get better and more affordable housing. Some children in this age group talk about getting Section 8, the government subsidy program, and explain that this is why people come to the shelter. They do not completely understand the concept of Section 8, but they possess essential pieces of information about it, such as it makes an apartment cost less.

Adolescents' Explanations

Adolescents report the reasons for their becoming homeless in a much more complex manner. Like the seven- to twelve-year-olds, they are very aware of the concrete indicators, for example, roaches, broken glass, dirt, and violence in their neighborhoods. They are also able to articulate classes of causes, such as drugs or lack of money. However, they are also able to see the interconnections between these causes and to conceptualize the whole picture. While their story may leave some loose ends, it is evident that they do have some sense that a "leaky roof," "too many roaches," "drugs all over our neighborhood," "a landlord who wouldn't do anything," and "not enough money" are causes that are somehow linked to one another. A twelve-year-old whose family had moved from another country described the complex interplay of reasons:

> We had to move because the owner kicked us out . . . because my mother didn't have a lot of money to pay the house. There was four of us living in the apartment. She run out of money because she had

to stop working because she was going to have a baby. And the money she had to pay for rent became higher, became 700 dollars. It used to be four or five or something like that. The place we were living was small because when we came here we didn't have a lot of money to get a big place. There was only three rooms. It had one bedroom and one side there was the kitchen and the other side there was the living room. It was pretty crowded. Well, one day, the owner came to our house and said that we had to move because we didn't pay and that he'll meet us at court. We went to court but the owner chickened out. He wasn't there. And then these two people, workers, helped us and said that we were going to move to a shelter so that we could get a cheaper, bigger apartment later on. The shelter would help us to get a paper to get a new apartment. (Raymond)

Beginning to see that the causes of homelessness are somehow interconnected, that causes are feeding into one another in a circular fashion, also begins to sharpen children's sense of awareness of the trap they are in. The interdependence of causes is often described in stories in which children see no way out. While children at this age do not specifically articulate the concept of being trapped, their stories may describe situations for which they perceive no solutions. The story of a twelve-year-old boy explaining how he and his mother repeatedly became homeless described the trap the child felt:

We were in a shelter because we didn't have enough money. The place I was at was in—a school for bad kids—was having my mom give up all her money that she had and she got, so she quit her job. Then we moved to the shelter, and then she got another job, and then we moved to the trailer park. That was the best place we ever lived because it was our own house. But then we couldn't stay living in there because we couldn't make any more payments. And we were far away from my mom's job, because she was working at the same job. The place she worked was far away. When I heard we had to move from there I didn't say anything. I never say anything. (Ryan)

Children at this stage are not only aware of the complexity of reasons by which they became homeless but also are aware of the complexity and subtleties of the bureaucratic system. They come to know that the system's rules operate in an awkward and often inflexible manner, and that they must bend to the demands of the system in order to get what they need. For example, Dana and Haydn, who have been living in a suburb with their father, both realize that their mother, who was just released from jail, cannot get subsidized housing, which she desperately needs, unless her children are living with her in the shelter. While they are angry at the way the system works, they are realistic about doing what they must to help their mother.

At this stage, children also may attribute some of the reasons for their homelessness to their parents. They believe that if their parents had acted in a different manner, they would not have to be homeless. In addition, they may offer an understanding of psychological contributors to their parent's situation. Amidst Ian's list of multiple and interacting reasons for homelessness (a welfare system that "stinks," uncaring grandparents, mother's divorce from stepfather), he included his impression that his mother "wasn't around me enough." He then concluded, "I think she's messed up, but just like any other mom."

Role of Insufficient Money

While the variety of reasons offered by children for becoming homeless is infinite, children of all ages begin to realize fairly quickly, in their different ways of reasoning, that they do not have enough money and that they are homeless because they are poor. Homelessness for them is directly related to a lack of money; if they were rich, they would not be homeless.

Their understanding of money is itself a developmental issue. How money works, that is, how one gets it, and what it is worth, are concepts that differ at different stages of development. The very young often include lack of money as one in a long list of factors seen as causing homelessness. Although money may be mentioned by young children, they are unable to elaborate how or why lack of money contributes to homelessness. For these children, money works magically. "Mommy goes to the bank and they give her money." "Mommy gets money by the check. She buys us stuff when she gets her check." There are no relative amounts. The concept of "enough money" is not part of their repertoire. Money is something you either have or you don't. And if you have it at all, you have plenty. Young children believe that the size of the pile of bills that one has is an indicator of the amount of money. As one girl explained:

My uncle is rich because he works at a popcorn place and if people buy popcorn from him he gets a lot of money. One day he took all

his money out and it was a bunch of money. . . . I can tell he's rich.
I see a lot of money. (Nancy)

Viewing money as magically obtained makes it difficult for young
children to understand why, if someone has money, they do not help
them.

As they mature, children begin to make a more explicit connection
between work and money. In a very concrete fashion, they attribute the
lack of money to lack of a job. Children at this stage make little or no
distinction between types of jobs and how much can be earned, nor do
they indicate an awareness that the availability of jobs is a potential
problem. They have little realization that one could work very hard and
still not have enough money. They perceive a one-to-one correspondence
between having money and being able to pay for everything. They believe
quite clearly that if their mother or daddy were working they would have
money and they would not be homeless. As one child stated, "They don't
got a house because they didn't go working. The people that doesn't have
a house maybe didn't work" (Raymond).

Older children and adolescents have developed a mature understanding
of money and how it works. They realize that even if one is working,
one can be poor and not have enough money to meet survival expenses.
They are also aware that it is difficult to find jobs and that some jobs pay
so little that they would not solve the family's problems. They are able
to put some perspective into the situation. Like other adolescents, T. J.
saw the connection between his family's homelessness and the fact that
his mother stopped working. Yet he also realized how difficult it was for
her to continue working while raising five children.

Far-reaching Explanations

Once they realize that becoming homeless only happens to some
families, indeed a minority of families, children develop some general
ideas about why some people get to be homeless and some do not. Unlike
older adolescents or adults, who might attribute their finding themselves
in this situation to bad luck or the way the cookie crumbled, young
children usually develop more personalized accounts of homelessness,
such as focusing on people doing bad things to them. "I don't know why
some people live in shelters and some don't. I think some people live
here because maybe the owner kicked them out. Maybe the owner kicked
them out" (Raymond).

As they get older, children begin to attribute homelessness to life's unfairness. A nine-year-old girl whose family was very poor and had lived in a series of substandard apartments before finally becoming homeless viewed her circumstances not only as fate but as some form of reverse punishment.

> It's funny that some people get to be homeless and some don't. The way I think is that the bad people, some bad people, they always have everything. And the good people, who want to be good to everybody, they try to be polite to one another, they always get the bad things done to them . . . I think that happens, because when you're good, things come out bad and when you're bad, things come out good. (Isabella)

Chapter Four

"Living Here's Not Bad but Not Good Enough": Shelter Living

ELIZABETH

Elizabeth is a thirteen-year-old sixth-grader. She is one of six children and is the sister of Ingrid whose story we heard earlier. Her mother is divorced from her father and receives no financial support from him. After falling behind on the rent, Elizabeth's family moved to the shelter five months ago.

I just turned thirteen. I'm in the sixth grade. I've been here about four or five months. I like it, except I just don't like it in the mornings because the kids all get up and they're running around and they're screaming and I can't get any rest really. Sometimes it's my brother and sister, but sometimes it's other kids too. But there's this one little kid here that wakes up with the birds and he just wakes up really early and he wakes up all the kids because he goes upstairs without his mother's permission and just screams his head off and then all the kids get up and start screaming around and everything. That's the worst part of living here. That and plus other people complaining. Like I was sick a couple days ago and I was eating cereal because I just wanted to eat something soft so I could digest it and everybody was complaining because I was eating the cereal. Everybody in the shelter was yelling at me and telling me that I should put it away because it's for breakfast in the morning and we only get a certain amount of it. I'm kind of upset about that.

And then they just treat this one girl, that's the same age as me, differently because she's bigger. She's just taller and she has more something. They treat her more respectfully than they treat me because when I was in the office one time talking on the telephone and one of the staff workers came here and told me to get out of the office but let the same girl talk in there and didn't say anything to her. And then another time was when this girl was downstairs and she told me I had to go to bed and me and her had the same time to go to bed and it's nine o'clock. She told me I had to go to bed and she didn't tell the other girl to go to bed. She just told me. They treat me like a little kid because I'm not as big as she is. But I always help them out. . . .

I don't like having no privacy. I got a bunch of birthday presents for my birthday and I had this one little balloon, a helium-filled balloon and it never would unflate unless somebody popped it. And I was going to keep it for a long time because I'm not going to be able to see my friend who gave it to me for a while because she's moving to Wyoming and I'm moving to Rochelle and so I wanted to keep that for a very long time and I put it really safe. I put it under my bed, where the kids never usually go. I put it under my bed with a blanket over it. But one little girl came in my room and was looking around. Her mother was looking for her shoe because the babies always take her shoes. She came in and she looked under my bed and she saw the balloon and she goes "Here, wanna play with the balloon!" and then the little girl, she popped it. I didn't know about it until I got home from school and I was wicked upset and so I only have a couple pieces of the balloon left to keep. That felt bad. But I still got something else that my friend gave me. I got a little bracelet.

When we left our first house, all our stuff, at least most of it, went in storage. But like our couches were all raggly and so we threw those away, our old ones. And the house we just moved out of was all furnished so it was okay. So we had to leave that stuff there. And then we left some of our plates and dishes there for the people, because my brother broke a lamp playing football. My big brother broke a little lamp. You know those lights that come down, that you just turn on the switch and all three lights come on? Well, he threw it really hard and it broke one of them. It just came down and broke. And then another one was a lamp, one of those ones that hangs from the ceilings. It has that wrapping around it and my brother was jumping off the fireplace and seeing if he could touch it and then he touched it and his whole finger went through it. And just pulled it down and it just ripped. And then another thing was that this girl, wanted to surprise me for my birthday and so I came home and she's trying to rearrange my room. It was all nicely rearranged and then I came home and it was all clean and I found a lamp broken. She moved the table and then stepped on a wire from the lamp. The lamp tipped and just fell over and broke. That was in the house we used to live in.

It's better living in your own house. You have more privacy. It's a lot more quieter. I get to talk on the phone longer with my friends that I'm going to miss. Here in the shelter I was mad because there's this one girl here that was upstairs talking on the phone for like forty-five minutes and then my friend called me and so she had to get off the phone so I could use it. I used it and they told me I had to get off after I was talking with her for three minutes. And my friend was calling me from long distance to talk to me. She lives in either Texas or Arizona, I forgot which one she lives in. And I could only talk to her for three minutes. That made me feel bad and mad. They just treat her more better than me, but she's just the same age as me and I get treated as a baby, like I'm a seven or six year old. I don't like it.

I think living in your own house is much better. You don't have to share a bathroom with somebody. When we share a bathroom with somebody my mother always buys the shampoo and everybody uses the shampoo and conditioner. Everybody always uses it and so it's all gone in like two days. In our new house, me and my sister will have our own bathroom. It's just me and her, so we have our own soap and everything. And in the shelter, you don't know what other people have been doing because one day a little boy pooped and his mother wiped it up with a cloth and then just washed it off with soap and water and then put it back on the sink for somebody to wash their hands with. I like a house better than living in a shelter. But I also like living in a shelter because you get to do a lot more things than you would at your house. You go on more trips than you would at home, like field trips. Sometimes you don't have enough time to do it, but it's fun sometimes. There's a lot of things you can do. They have a lot of things for kids. And it's close to some of my friends that live around here. I like that too. My friends have been over here but only three of them though. No, I think five or six of my friends have been over here, but the rest are usually busy. When they come over they think it's nice. They think that all the people here are nice. . . .

We had to move out of our house. That's why we came here. We got evicted because my mother didn't have enough money to pay rent and because my father wasn't giving us a lot of child support and because he couldn't afford it because he has to give it to three other girls too—his girlfriends from before. No, I think he only has to give it to my mom, this other girl and another girl. And so he didn't have enough money to keep paying us child support and so he never gave us child support and my mother was the only one working because my brother quit his job. He got fired of his job because he came late for work a lot of times. He worked at the gas station and then my mother didn't have enough money to pay rent all of the time, so the lady used to help us out but then they ran out of money and we got evicted out of our house because we didn't have enough money to pay the rent for our house. I was kind of happy a little bit because I was coming here and I was happy because we were moving out of that house. That house was just falling apart. When we moved in the washer and the dryer broke and my mother had to pay for it and we didn't even use it. And the dishwasher was broken and the lights were breaking and then they left this one switch on, and they didn't tell us what it was for. They said it was for a light. We turned it on and it blew every fuse in our house and the house was just falling apart and there was bugs galore and I just didn't like it. There was one floor of the attic and then another floor but it was downstairs and it was like a basement a little bit. It was a bunch of rooms and all the time we'd get potato bugs. All we'd get was potato bugs and it was just scary because at night you would have to bring a flashlight and stuff with you so you don't step on the bugs. And it was just really gross. So I was glad to move. Before I saw the shelter, I thought it was going to be small. It's pretty big. And I thought it was going to be much quieter. I never thought it would be this noisy. But, I like it. The kids are noisy though, the little kids. And in the morning the people making breakfast so you hear ting ting ting. And everybody getting up to go to school and, it's just really noisy. . . .

Sometimes around here, when I get really frustrated, I just go up to my room and I sit and read. I escape. I get frustrated here a lot. Sometimes like I'll be busy and somebody will ask me to watch their kids for them and I just say "I can't right now" and they get mad and I just feel really bad so I do it for them anyway. And then their kids turn into brats and I just can't handle it anymore, I say "I can't watch them anymore" and I go upstairs because I can't handle it sometimes. It's too much. And one person here, Mary, has a little son named Kyle, and he just drives me up the wall because he's always running around screaming. So he just drives me up a wall. And a couple of days ago my alarm clock went off for no reason, and so he goes "Oh fire, fire" and then he was just all night and all day going "Eeeh eeeh" and "Fire, fire." And I was just frustrated. Everybody told him to "Please be quiet." He just did it at night. And he gets up in the middle of the night. Everybody will be asleep and he'll go "Mommy!" and all the kids wake up and I'll have to go upstairs and put the kids back to sleep for my mom. Last night I was making cupcakes for a celebration I was having today and he came out and he was crying because his mother wasn't here doing her sewing. And he comes out and starts banging on the door. And I go "Come on Kyle go to bed." And I picked him up and I put him to bed. And he comes up and he goes "Mom!" and then all the kids woke up in the house. All you hear is "Aaaaaahhh." Tatyana was crying, my bother and sister woke up, everybody woke up, and I had to put the kids back to sleep so I never got a chance to finish my cupcakes until late that night.

NANCY

Nancy, who is ten, lives in the shelter with her eleven-year-old brother and her mother, who is nine months pregnant. They have been here for three weeks. They left their home because of marital difficulties and stayed in the home of a friend for a few weeks. Their father is still in the area.

I have a brother and he's eleven years old and I'm ten years old. We've been here for a week at this shelter. It's the first time we ever came to a shelter. I like it. It's excellent. I like to live here more than any other place ever. I like it. You can do a lot of stuff here like games, coloring, watching TV. The lady here, the boss, tells you when to go to bed and get up. She tells you so you're never late for school. I'm still going to the same school as when I lived at my house. The kids in school still think I'm living at my house. I told my principal and teacher that I live at the shelter now. I said I still wanted to go to that school. I thought I'd have to go to another school. I was glad, real glad, that I didn't have to move to another school.

I didn't know what the shelter was going to be like before I came. I thought it was going to be old and junky and have all new rules. I thought it was going to be a big gymnasium with cots and everything. I just felt mad. I started to get used to it the first night and liked it a lot. I wanted to stay at my mother's friend's house till we got our apartment. I didn't want to come here. All three of us have one room, that's good. I like being in the same room as my mommy. I like being with my brother too. It's not so scary that way. My brother's fun to play with. There's one girl that I didn't want to be my friend. She's got a baby—a boy and a girl. I don't like the girl. She stole one of our colored pencils and never gave it back. We have fun at the lounge when she's not there to bother us. I like our room. It's right near the bathroom. We get snack food too, because we're near the kitchen.

I don't want to tell kids in school where I live because my mother doesn't want them to know because they'll make fun of us. My friends wouldn't like me anymore. They'd make fun because we're living here and we're not in a normal house. They'd say "You're not normal and you're not in a normal house. You're in a shelter." My friends think I'm living in our house still. They ask to sleep over and I say no. Some of them know I'm not in my house. They think we're just living in a house, another house, not a shelter.

The best part of living here is playing school. It's easier to get breakfast. The bad part is we can't have Nintendo. We left it at our house. But it feels better living here than in our other house. There was all fighting and stuff. Our father was fighting my mother. It was awful most of the time. It was real awful. We're going to be here until we can get an apartment. We came here a month ago I think.

There's a lot of rules here. We have to be in bed at nine. I don't like it. In our apartment we can stay up as late as we want. The rules are different from our own apartment. We get our own room in the apartment, but not here. And in your own apartment, there's no certain time for snacks. Here you can only have snacks at certain times that the people here say. In our own apartment, we don't have to be out of the kitchen at a certain time. We can have snacks whenever we want. You can have as much cereal as you want in your own place. Here, some things in the refrigerator have names on them and we can't have it. And some of these things I like. If we get three warnings here we have to go. At home we don't get kicked out. You get to cook supper at home whenever you want and you can cook whatever you want. At the shelter you have to eat at a certain time and only the food that they cook. Sometimes I don't like it at all. In your own house you can watch movies, and stay up and have popcorn and chips. Here, you can't eat in the lounge or in your room. You can't have slumber parties here either. You can't even jump on your bed. The lady boss gets mad if you do. At your own apartment, you can make a mess in your room if you want to. You can have the radio as loud as you want.

Here it's not so good. We have to be with our mother at all times here. Here, we can't get in from outside if we don't ring the bell. At home, we don't have to ring a bell to get in your own house. At home, we don't have to go back and forth to the office for every little thing. And, what I really don't like in the shelter is you can't always watch what you want on TV. At home you can go into any refrigerator anytime you want to. And you can go in anyone's room. Here there's a staff refrigerator that you can't go in and you can't go in other people's rooms. And in your own apartment, you don't have to leave your shoes on at all times. They tell you everything in the shelter, what you can and what you can't do, what time you have to go to bed and eat your food. At home you can go outside and play in the yard. You can't here. There's not even no yard.

Mostly here, my brother and me, we don't like "the rules." The worst thing is what we can't do. But it's not bad really. First night my brother was angry. We came late at night. He felt very sad. This made mom feel sad. We cried. We didn't know what to do. We just cried.

COMMENTARY

In their stories, Nancy and Elizabeth describe, in significant detail, the frustrating aspects of shelter living. They are also aware of the positive parts of shelter life. And although they would rather not live in a shelter, both see some reasons why living in a shelter is in some ways a better alternative to their previous existence. Most homeless children have similar lists of likes and dislikes, and nearly all have mixed feelings about living in a shelter.

Once they have arrived in the shelter, it is normal for children quickly to become aware of the pluses and minuses of shelter living. Through clearly articulating these likes and dislikes, children express their feelings about shelter living. Most children have a longer list of dislikes than likes. The long list of complaints, while real, is another way of saying "I do not like being here."

As might be expected, the younger children are more likely to articulate their likes and dislikes in concrete terms (for example, rotten vegetables), while older children tend to describe more general characteristics of the living situation (for example, no choice of food). Many children complain about very specific characteristics of the shelter that they find different from what they knew at home, such as the food, telephone arrangements, and space. Marcus' list of complaints is typical of many children's reactions to living in a shelter. He said that he is bored in the shelter, is prevented from playing how and where he wants to, and that he is bothered watching TV because of noise or because someone else controls the channel. He described the food as spoiled, other people at the shelter as mean, and the beds as uncomfortable. He also emphasized the pest problem:

There's too many bugs. Like ants, and spiders, and mosquitos. All the bugs come from outside. There's cracks and they come through the cracks. And roaches. The roaches come from the cracks when they smell food. I seen the roaches. I kill them. I take my shoe and hit them. They run.

Such concerns about bugs are mentioned repeatedly in the stories of these children. Many children, particularly those between seven and eleven years of age, seem extremely troubled by the presence of bugs in the shelter. The presence of bugs seems to concretize for these children all that they perceive as negative about the shelter.

Living Close to Others

Predictably, many of the dislikes in the shelter revolve around living close to other people. Many children are aware that they do not like this aspect of the shelter, but cannot explain why. Twelve-year-old Ryan could only describe it as, "I don't like having other people around. I just think it's hard. I don't know why it's hard, but it is hard though." Other children describe it as difficult and scary, and believe that the strangers with whom they are forced to live will hurt them. Jose expressed concerns about this issue when telling of his arrival at the shelter: "When I first came here, I was scared. It was strange. I thought they were bad people that would try to make friends with me and get me in trouble. There were a lot of people I didn't know."

Living with such a large number of people is often difficult for the younger children, for whom family boundaries are more diffuse. At home, they might have been one of four or six people. Now they are one of thirty or fifty, and their identity is threatened. Who they are and who their family is may be difficult concepts to hold on to, particularly when many people, such as staff, other mothers, or older children, are doing the mothering.

The large number of people living in the shelter tends to make life institutional and somewhat impersonal. It becomes difficult for children and adolescents to satisfy their need for nurturance and to be cared for as a child. The structure of the shelter is designed for the many, with few or no special arrangements for individuals. This is pointedly evident in Elizabeth's story, in which she describes her struggle to get cereal when she was sick.

The difficulty adjusting to living with a large number of people is amplified by the presence of so many children. Interacting with the other children living in the shelter can be a difficult challenge for most children. This is especially true when each child is competing for a limited amount of resources, be it the television or the nurturance of adults. For many older children, the number of younger children is problematic. Because there are proportionately many more younger than older children in the shelters, older children can often feel isolated and overwhelmed by "little kids." Having one or two little brothers or sisters pestering you can now be increased to fifteen or twenty younger children. Children and adolescents repeatedly complain of having "too many little kids around" and not enough of their peer group. Even Sean, who is just six, reported:

> I don't like kids bothering me. They come up to me and talk to me while I'm watching TV. And they come hit me. They come hit me with the toys. They're little kids. Now they moved, they moved out of here. There's only one kid here like me, he's seven, but he's not here. He moved outta here. He was six but he turned seven. There's no other big kids here, just me and my brother and Doug, but Doug's not here yet, he's coming tomorrow.

Conversely, for some of the younger children, a shelter with many teenagers can also be difficult. Vicky, who is eight, described her frustration: "The other kids are nice. But some of them are annoying. They make noises that makes me run up a wall. And, they bother us. And all the bigger kids who are older than me call us like wimps and stuff because we won't try stuff. They are mean."

Noise

Another consequence of living close to a large number of other people is having to tolerate a significant amount of noise. Children often spontaneously comment on how noisy the shelter is. Many children report that the noise of TV and radios is a source of much frustration to them and their parents. An adolescent girl reported:

> It's like the next door neighbor in unit twelve, I think, is real noisy. Like at night she waits until nine o'clock and turns up her radio, her TV and I'm in bed and I can't go to sleep. And once my mother went outside and went to her door and said, "Turn down that TV. My children's trying to sleep." I don't know what she said back because I was inside trying to go to sleep. (Stephanie)

Living close to other people exposes one's own and others' personal habits. Frequently, children and adolescents report that other people have habits or behaviors that infringe upon their personal style or are outright offensive. This is especially true for adolescents, for whom issues of hygiene are becoming particularly important. Ian complained that

> Some of the people who live here are gross. . . . It's just that some of the people smell. Like, like they clean the baby in the bathroom sink. Like they're just dirty. Why can't you just do it like every other normal person, just use wipes and stuff. It's weird. We go crazy.

Jose described his dislike for the behavior of the people in the shelter:

> I don't like the other people here too much. Sometimes, they get in trouble. Like if they spank their kids or something they get in trouble. If the people here see them, or if they give their kids away, or if they get four warnings from here, they have to go somewhere else. You get warnings if you talk bad and fight and that stuff.

The personal habits of other people are not only distasteful; these habits or behaviors can also threaten children's sense of identity. Living with other people with whom they share the current circumstance of homelessness can lead children to question whether they share their characteristics. This can often be quite threatening to children, who do not want to be identified with people who behave in ways they find distasteful, but who nevertheless are associated with them because they are part of the group in that shelter. In their uncertainty, children attempt to make pointed distinctions between themselves and the others in the shelter. Vicky, for example, reported: "The other mothers, they're mean to the kids and they tell them to go to sleep and they wouldn't and then they spank them. My mom never spanks me."

Fighting

Living close to others also contributes to increased interpersonal tension. This results in frequent fighting. While some of the fighting is overt, most occurs in the form of backbiting and people taking sides against one another. In the shelters, where guests share common living areas, such as the TV room, kitchen, and play areas, the proximity exacerbates normal tensions between people, particularly strangers. Robert Frost's warning that "good fences make good neighbors" cannot be heeded in an environment where sharing living space is a requirement for survival. Even young children are aware of this problem. While fighting among children occurs in any environment, a housed child in conflict with a friend has the option of picking up his toys and going home. Children in shelters are afforded no such escape route. Opportunities for these children to disengage in order to "cool off" are limited. Mario, who is four years old, says that what he doesn't like about the shelter is "having to be in bed too early and fighting with other kids." Seven year old Charlie, who lived with his mother in a motel said:

> The worst part of living here is having friends fighting against you. Like, the kid that lives across the parking lot. Every time he comes over here he fights against me and then we go over there and I kick the ball up in the air, my ball, and he just, whenever I catch it he just pushes me down and all that.

Confinement

One of the aspects of the shelter that many children find difficult is the confining nature of the building. Shelters are often located in urban areas in large institution-like buildings. There is usually little or no yard space, and very little interior play area for the children. Consequently, children feel restricted to staying inside the building, even on warm summer days. Marcus reported:

> I don't like staying up in the house all day. But when I go out and play in the parking lot, Dan comes out and says we make too much noise. Dan works here. We can't play in the street because my mother won't let me because I might get hit. We can play in the garden. That's OK. I don't like it here.

Children are further confined by limited access to a telephone. For children without transportation, the phone is often their only means to contact friends or other family members. Understandably, the line for the phone is usually long, and once the phone is obtained, conversations must be kept brief. Shelters typically have pay phones, and children repeatedly note the impossibility of making a call without having "a lot of change money."

Rules

Many children complain about the rules that regulate aspects of shelter or motel living. While each institution specifies its own rules, the shared living arrangements in the shelters seem to make necessary a number of regulations concerning meals, bedtime, use of TV and radio, showers, curfews, visitors, access to transportation, noise, and discipline of children. The children often find the rules burdensome.

Many of the rules about which the children complain are those that contribute to blurring the age differences between children. For example, many children resent a rule stating that all children must be in bed at a certain hour. Older children would like the rule to accommodate their relative age, and argue that they should not have to be in bed at the same time as their younger sibling. The fine distinctions that can be made in one's own family, for example between a ten-year-old and a seven-year-old, disappear in a large group where the major distinction is between children and adults.

Children also resent rules that infringe on activities about which there are no rules at home, for example, watching TV. They dislike rules that restrict or limit what would otherwise be normal behavior. Isabella described the dilemma of having to follow shelter rules:

> I don't like nothing about watching English TV when I don't want to and I want to watch Spanish TV instead. And I have to go to bed at eight o'clock. I don't know why I have to go to bed at eight o'clock. It's the rule of the shelter. When I was home I went to bed at ten. Being in a shelter you have to follow those rules in a shelter by the leader and in my home, I do what my mother says, but here they do different rules and I'm not used to different rules.

Likewise Kendra noted that:

> You get to do whatever you want when you live at home, but at a place like this you can't do anything you want, because they have rules. And you have to go by the rules. But when you're in your own house, you do what you want to do. If I have to be in, it's because my father tells me what time to be in. You don't have to be in when people tell you to.

Both Isabella and Kendra are aware of the differences between the rules that their parents have made and the rules of the shelter. This dichotomy is often difficult for young children to understand. Some children are disturbed by their mother's authority being usurped. Tara expressed this when she stated that a home is a place where "my mother doesn't have to do what people tell her to. Here they tell her to always do her chores, and I always think that's dumb."

Older children resent the fact that the autonomy they have earned is taken away from them. Fourteen-year-old Dana stated: "It's hard here because of the certain hours we have to be in. Because at my father's, he says we're grown up and we can make our own time to come in." Other older children learn to capitalize on the rule differences. Sometimes, if the shelter's rule is more lenient, they tend to play the difference to their advantage. T. J., who is seventeen, has figured out the positive aspects of the discrepancy in the rules:

> When I first came here, they told me that my curfew would probably be around my mother's curfew for me. But it turned out to be later here. I don't think my mother would have me coming in that late. Really, I don't think she would. She's only going along with it because it's the rule here. And I would probably have a fuss if she didn't.

One of the rules of the shelter that is particularly bothersome to children involves who can visit or stay overnight in the shelter. These rules are intended to protect the privacy and limited living space of the families who live at the shelter, but they often serve as barriers to visitors whom the children would like to see.

Many shelters have rules about who in the family is allowed to live in the shelter, often accepting only women and children. Consequently, any men who may be in the family are required to stay somewhere else. The children's father and/or their mother's husband or live-in boyfriend become separated from the family. Children who find their family separated in this way describe it as a very negative aspect of the shelter.

Better than the Alternative

While most children express intense dislike of some aspects of shelter living, they also speak positively about many aspects of the shelter. Most of what they like about the shelter is what they consider to be an improvement over their living situation prior to coming to the shelter. For some children, the shelter is better than the alternative that was available to them. They find some things about the shelter that address previously unmet, or inadequately met, needs. There are some children who are clearly very pragmatic about the benefits of living in the shelter, particularly with respect to providing for their basic needs, such as food. Many report that the good part of the shelter is that it brings increased access to permanent housing. They know that moving into the shelter is a way to speed up the process of their receiving a state certificate for subsidized housing. "The good part of living here is it's how you get a good apartment fast."

Children see other positive dimensions of the shelter as well. Tucker enumerated some of these benefits:

> I like it here because it's got a playroom and it's got crayons and it's got beds. Before I didn't have a real bed. We used to live at my grandmother's house and we didn't have enough money for beds yet and we used to sleep on these little chair beds like you see at the store. Well, I'd sleep on one, Bethany would sleep on the couch, and my mom would sleep on another couch. We used to sleep on things that represent beds. I like it here. You get a couple of blankets here! Like you get a quilt, and then you get one blanket. Then you get a couple sheets. We didn't have that where we lived before. We used to have a sheet over us. That's it. I used to wrap it all around me. I was cold.

Younger children describe very concrete aspects of the shelter that they like. "All the toys" is an immediate positive for these children, particularly in those shelters where there are a number of toys available for the group. Young children are particularly enthusiastic in the few shelters that have the luxury of an organized play group or on-site formal day-care program. Five-year-old Doreen listed "the toys, a computer, and two television sets," which were in the day-care room, as reasons why she liked living in the shelter.

More opportunities for nurturance constitute another positive aspect of the shelter for many children. The presence of many caretakers, such as other mothers, older children, and shelter staff, may provide increased nurturance for some children, particularly if their living circumstances prior to coming to the shelter had made it difficult for the mother to be nurturing. One young child, who prior to coming to the shelter, had to take significant responsibility for himself and his sisters, said that the shelter was good "because the staff woke you up so that you got to school on time." One positive aspect of the shelter for twelve-year-old Jose was that "We get happy here because men sometimes bring us to the library and let us take a book out. And they help us with homework. When I have homework I just go downstairs in the office and they'll help you with it. A lady downstairs helps especially." Many children become very attached to the staff who provide the children with a significant amount of individual attention. In spite of the strained circumstances under which they work, many staff find considerable time and energy to respond to the individual needs and requests of children.

For some children, the presence of other people in the shelter constitutes a support. Children become friendly with other children and mothers, and often spend time together. Sometimes, other mothers can help mediate family disputes, or may simply provide a new perspective on a troublesome family issue. Some children are quite aware how good it is for their mother to have made friends with other mothers in the shelter. This is particularly true where mothers have been isolated and have not received much social support prior to coming to the shelter. One nine-year-old boy reported: "The best thing about the shelter is that my mother made a friend. She never really had anyone to talk to before. Now we do stuff together" (Tucker). This child is clearly aware of the social support the shelter provides for his mother.

Ambivalent Feelings

Beyond their list of likes and dislikes in the shelter, most children can express in a very direct manner their feelings about having to live in a shelter. A relatively small number of children express very clear and unambivalent feelings, either very positive or very negative, about being in the shelter. For a few children, the shelter represents a significantly better arrangement to their former living situation. These children describe the contrast between the difficult circumstances in which they lived and the more positive circumstances of the shelter. They are enthusiastic about the shelters: "I like it here. It's excellent. It's real excellent." But, for another few children, the shelter represents the worst of all possible situations. These children express clear and very negative feelings about the shelter. They dislike it intensely, see no redeeming features of any part of shelter living, and hate being constrained to live there: "It's sad and it's just bad" (Jose).

Most children's feelings, however, are neither completely positive nor negative. The shelter represents something of a mixed blessing. On the one hand, they know they have come to a low point in their lives. Living in the shelter has a significant number of undesirable characteristics. "Kids think it's bad, just bad." But on the other hand, arriving at a shelter provides a certain amount of relief to a number of children. It concretizes the realization that they have some place to stay, particularly when many of them had imagined that their circumstances could result in their living on the street. And living in the shelter itself has some positive dimensions. On a day-to-day basis, they do not perceive it as all bad. This ambivalence about the shelter and shelter living is evident in the phrases children use to describe how they feel about living in a shelter: "Living here's not bad but it's not good enough" (Jose). "I don't know if I like living here, sometimes 'ya' sometimes 'no.' It's not too bad but I'd rather live somewhere else" (Dana).

It is clear from their stories that most homeless children have mixed feelings about day-to-day life in a shelter. They are well aware of its pluses and minuses. But none of them are ambivalent about the bottom line: the shelter is an unacceptable place to live because it simply is not home. Adolescents articulated this sentiment most clearly: "The worst part of the shelter is just the fact of being here. It's just not wanting to be here. I'd tell another kid who was coming that he's going to feel sad and stuff about not having a home" (Juan). And Ian stated: "The worst part of living in a shelter is just not having an apartment, not having your own house to live in. Having to live in a shelter, that's the worst part."

There is no ambivalence for any of these children about the real constraint in their lives, that is, being forced to live in a shelter in the first place. It is this inescapable demand that constitutes, for homeless children, an unequivocally awful burden.

Chapter Five

"I Had to Leave Some Stuff Behind": Loss and Disappointment

HAYDN

Sixteen-year-old Haydn came to the shelter with his brother Dana. His parents divorced six years ago and the boys remained with their mother for several years until they moved in with their father, stepmother, and six step-siblings. They lived there for four years, during which time their mother was incarcerated on drug-related charges. Their mother was recently released from prison and the decision was made that the boys join her in the shelter to help her get back on her feet.

I'm sixteen years old. I've been at the shelter a week or so. I was living with my dad in Fairhale. But I came here to the shelter to help my mother. I came so I could help my mom get a place to stay. That's why we came to live here because we're supposed to be with her in order for her to get a place. She can't get a place unless we're with her because she needs to have kids to get the rent certificate. We were living with my dad I'd say about four years. Before that I was with my mom. I was always with my mom and dad until they broke up. I was about ten when they broke up. I was living in the city. And they broke up and then my dad moved to Riverside. Then I went and stayed with my dad for a while in Riverside and then came back to my mom for a while. Then my dad went to Fairhale and I was still living with my mom and my dad asked me did I want to come live with him and I said "yeah." And my mother let me go. And then I was with him for a while and my mother got into trouble and she went to jail for a while and then I came here to the shelter. She got into trouble a while after I went to live with my dad. I want to live with my dad, but I had to help my mother out. I decided I had to. My dad thinks I should come help my mother out. And he was here yesterday. He told me any time I want to come back, I can come back. Any time. That makes me feel good. . . .

I really like living with my father. He has his wife, my stepmother, and he has six kids. One's just got born, my baby brother, Matty. He's not even two months yet. And, my other brother, Joe, he's two or three, and my other little brother, Dean is four. Then there's my sister, Sarah and my other brothers, Peter and Justin. I think that's five, no six. . . .

Here at the shelter, it's not too bad, but I'd rather live somewhere else. It's not that hard for me but I would rather live with my father in my own house and my own room and my own things. I'd just rather have it like that. Living in a place like this is totally different from living in your own place. You have little or no privacy. It's just weird, because when you want to get up and go to the bathroom, you're used to seeing your own family. But then getting up, going to the bathroom here, you're like totally seeing different people. It's weird. There's two bathrooms here, one upstairs and one downstairs. So it's like you see different people at night going to the bathroom. I just don't like it. Other stuff too is different from living in your own place. Here, I eat dinner with my mother. My mother fixes our dinner, but other people are sitting down eating dinner at the same table. I feel weird. I'm just used to my father and my other little brothers at the dinner table with me. The environment is totally different. You feel much more comfortable when you're eating with just your family.

I can deal with it, but I just don't want to deal with it. Some of these people are going to live here for totally long periods of time and I don't want to be. People are here a long time. I have no idea why. They choose not to help themselves. They don't do things to get places and settle down and get stable. My mother will be here for a while, but she's just like totally lost. Before she wasn't even doing drugs. She had a nice decent job at Northrop Corporation. She had a nice job, a car, a place to stay and things like that. We were there. My father was there. Then when my father left she still had the job and the car. And then, after we left to go to my father's, it seemed like she had nobody else and things were falling apart. She didn't do the drugs and the drinking until after we left. When we came back then she was doing it and we went back to live with my father. That was pretty rough.

She was doing all kinds of things, like drinking and doing a little bit of drugs, a lot of that stuff. I knew. I knew that she was doing it. My father knew it too. But when she went to jail, I think that her mind really got lost. She used to write us and I used to write back. She used to write to my father and my father used to write back to her. We kept pretty much in touch. She used to call and stuff. We never visited her there, never. We wrote her. I didn't want to go there, but we went there to deliver clothes and presents on Christmas and stuff like that. But I never saw her in there. I wanted to see her, but I just don't want to go in a place like that. I just don't like it. The worst part of having my mother in jail was just knowing my mother was in jail. Just knowing.

And like, my stepmother, she's a nice lady. Kids like me, if they have a stepmother, they always hate a little something about them. Even though I hate a little something about her, too, otherwise she was a nice lady. It was just like "She's a nice lady." But, just knowing my mother was in jail was hard. Kids used to ask me about my mother. Like if I was at school and I called my stepmother to pick me up, they'd say "Who's coming to pick you up?" and I go "My mother," but I meant my stepmother, not my real mother. So I think about that sometimes. It's kind of hard. The kids never said anything because I never told kids anything like that. I never said a word. Only my best friends I told stuff to, but not anything about my mother, my real mother. I told nothing on her.

My friends don't really know where I am now. I told one of my best friends I was going to stay at Renthrop with my mother. That's all I said. I didn't say nothing else. There's no need to say anything else. When I feel sad about things, I don't tell no one. I'm just telling the truth. I keep everything to myself. If I want to tell, it's only if I think it's the right time to say something and I've been holding it in for a while. Then I say something, but otherwise I don't say anything. I can tell my father because he knows when I'm mad and he knows when I'm happy. Sometimes he says, "What's the matter with you? You've been acting kind of weird lately." And I'll tell him and he can tell me some things and tell me things that are right and things that are wrong. But, otherwise I just keep it to myself. . . .

Living here, it's alright, but some things aren't alright. The people here are very nice, the people who live here and the people who work here. They're very nice. But it's just nothing compared to your own family. The other day we went to the amusement park. Usually, when we go to an amusement park, it's me and Dana and my father. We go with our family, it's just our family. But at the shelter, you're going with all different people. There's no harm in that, because it's just like school, but you know the kids in school, because you've been around them for three years and four years and you know the kids. But at the shelter, you're going somewhere else with people you don't even know and you don't know if you really trust them or not. It's like weird. Me and my brother share a room. My mother has her own room. But it's not like my own room at my father's. I still have it, but it's nothing like my own room. I have my own things and here I can't put anything in the room with my brother in there and I like to have my own things. Me and my brother don't like the same things. Some things we like the same, but some things we don't.

My brother, who's here in the shelter, lived with me in Fairhale with my father. My father adopted him when he was small, so he calls him "Dad." He is his dad, really, because he took him when he was small, when he was a baby. He adopted him when he was real, real small. So me and my brother were together the whole time. He never talks about my mom and jail and stuff. My brother's quiet about those things. He doesn't say anything about it. But, if you ask him he'll tell you. . . .

I miss my friends. They got that same attitude of "no drugs." A lot of them drive, too, so they don't drink or nothing. We go out to the movies and do fun stuff. I hang around mostly with those kids. We're always into activities. Like, we all have memberships at the health club. We all go there to play basketball and spend about an hour with bench weights and stuff like that. I kind of miss that since I came to the shelter, but my father told me I could come back any time. He came here yesterday. He says he likes the place here. Of course, he's not that type of guy. He doesn't even like being around this type of place. He likes to have his own place, own privacy, own house, own car, everything. He's a construction worker. He's a hard worker. My stepmother is a teacher. She works really hard. She's going to open up her own day care. She has a license and everything. My brother Dana didn't want to come here either. He just wanted to stay there where we were. It's a little harder on him because he's younger. He doesn't understand. When most things were happening in our family I was a little bit older. He was probably too young to understand. . . .

I don't tell any of my friends where I live. There's no need to tell where I live. I just tell them I live in Renthrop. They don't know it's a shelter. I don't tell because like any kids my age, I'd be ashamed. You just don't want your friends to know that you live in a shelter. I'd be ashamed of kids knowing that I got no place to stay. It doesn't feel right telling your friends, "Oh yeah, I live in a shelter." Because they'd tell your other friends and other friends start talking and it would get around and you get jerks that like to make fun of you and stuff like that. So it's not good at all to tell. I wouldn't tell my teachers neither. I would never tell my teachers things like that. I'm not that close to my teachers. I'd tell nobody in school. I'm pretty much going to leave it a secret. I'm ashamed of being here. Knowing that your mother doesn't have a place to stay and that you're here with no place to stay out in Renthrop and you don't know anybody and you don't have a place to stay—it feels horrible, it's a horrible feeling.

All those feelings, I just keep them trapped inside. I get mad once in a while, but, pretty much I just stay to myself. Sometimes I get sad but I keep that to myself too. I'm like my dad. He doesn't show too much emotion. When he gets angry, he's angry. That's where I get my temper. I got a quick temper. I get mad real quick. But I haven't been angry since I came to the shelter.

Before I came here I thought it was going to be like going to a shelter. A big, big place with a lot of people. I thought it was going to be one big room. I had no idea, really. I was worried when I came here. I was worried about people, man, about how people would act. I thought those people at the shelter, they don't care about anybody but themselves. They could care less about other people. I thought they were people who don't even socialize and stuff like that. But it wasn't that way. There are nice people here, real nice people here. If I know kids who have to come to a shelter, I'll tell them to try to make the best of it, to try to get along with people.

GEORGIA

Georgia is thirteen years old and in the eighth grade. She has an older sister and a younger sister. This is her family's first experience in a shelter; they have been here for six months. Prior to coming to the shelter they were living in a rented residence. Georgia's father is a recovered alcoholic who has been sober since she was five years old. When Georgia was ten years of age, her parents divorced. Her mother subsequently became involved with another alcoholic. She has been seeing him off and on for over two years. Since the divorce, Georgia's mother has had trouble paying the bills. Her father is no longer working. Georgia has had a significant amount of counseling to help her manage in the family situation.

I'm thirteen and I'm in the eighth grade. I've been in the shelter for almost seven months, and I'm ready to go. I have been here for a couple weeks now. I have a real problem accepting things. I come from an alcoholic background, with my father and my mother being co-dependent and I've always taken everything on my own shoulders. I'm not the oldest, but I'm middle. I was a little mother so to speak to my older sister and to my younger sister. So having to live here and having not just my mother tell me what to do, but having seven other people and staff, I just, at first I really, really lost it. I was feeling like saying, "You people cannot even tell me what to do. You're not even blood-related. You don't have any right." And I've always been a very demanding person. I like to be in control of everything that I do. I've had a lot of control in the past, until I got here. With my mother being co-dependent, she was always at her Al-Anon meetings and I was at home with my little sister and I set down the rules for her. And for my older sister, I gave her the rules even.

I was like the mother. And coming here it's like "Ah!" We had to come here because, the way I see it, my mother didn't really know what she was doing. She couldn't find any work. Either that or she wouldn't. She said she couldn't, I say she wouldn't. And we ran out of money. I felt that she wasn't trying hard enough. But I can understand that even if she did have a job, it would have been really difficult. But I see it as a lot of her fault.

My father used to drink but he's been sober for eight years. So that's really helpful. So, it's not his drinking that made us come to the shelter. He and my mother have been separated for three years now. I was five when he got sober. And then he was working. He had his own furniture business. And then, they were together for three more years until I was nine or ten or around then. Then my father had an affair. And that kind of broke them up. My mother was kind of shocked about that. She went into a really big depression. Not really big, but she felt really bad. She was kind of really down. She kept on trying to tell my father, because she was totally dependent on him, totally. She was always telling him "Well you know you can come back whenever you want to. You'll always have a home. You'll always have a place in my heart, bla bla" and all this stuff. And all the time I'm sitting on the sidelines thinking "God you're weak." You know, this was my mother, which is part of the reason why I think I'm very strong-willed. I'm a very strong person. And I think I get that not only because of my father, because I do have an alcohol personality. I just know I do because I have the same personality that my father had when he was drunk. Whenever my mother got really upset with me she'd say "You have the same personality your father did when he was drunk." I'm very demanding just as he is. I have a bad temper. It's kind of hard to put into words, but I just know if I pick up a drink that I will be an alcoholic. I already know that. It's just a feeling that I have inside. I have a deadly fear of alcohol and drugs. I saw what it could do. I know that I more or less would be one. The majority of kids of alcoholics are. I already know that I will. I just know it. I saw a program on TV. I believe if somebody said it, it probably would be true. And not just that. With my mother, she's really co-dependent. She gives up easily. She doesn't like to try new things. She makes the same mistakes. I mean, everybody makes mistakes, and I'm well aware of that, but she makes the same ones over and over and over again. And I'm not like that. If I mess up once, that's it.

Like with her boyfriend, Mark. The past two years they've been going out on and off, seeing each other. And he lived with us like five months after they met, he lived with us. And it was total disaster because he's an alcoholic, an active alcoholic, which put me in a major depression. My mother kind of forgot about me and spent all of her time pleasing him. Now that she didn't have my father, she did everything for him. And she totally forgot about me. I was just there to babysit Janet. That's my younger sister. One day, she just walked in the door and said, "Here's Janet." Then she'd be out the door all the time. She wouldn't be home until eleven o'clock or so. So that built up a lot of resentment against him because he was the symbol of me losing my house, because my mother wanted to move out of the house that we were in so she could move in with him. He tried to be my father and he took my mother away from me. So whenever I see him, all these resentments come flooding over me and I'm like "Aaah." And then I look at my mother and more or less the same resentments come up because she let him take her away from me. She let him convince her to give up the house that we had been living in for eight years where I had the only security I had had all my life.

So that's why we gave up the house. My mother says also that even at that time we were in debt and she wasn't keeping the mortgage up. But my father moved in and he had the house for almost two years before he finally lost it. So there wasn't really a reason to immediately get out. It was basically, she just used that as an excuse. It's basically because of Mark, because she wanted to start over fresh with him. She didn't want to be in the same house. Which I can understand, but I just wish it wasn't with him. They're not still going together now. At this time they're broken up. They broke up like three days ago. But when we move out of here, he was going to move with us again. But before when he did it was a total nightmare. When he walked in the room, I walked out of the room. I stopped talking to my mother, no communication. The only way we communicated was threats. It was terrible. And I'm only thirteen. That's hard to go through all that. Everybody thinks I'm more than thirteen, not only because of my parents, but after they get to know me it really blows their mind. Everybody thinks my maturity is definitely up a few years.

My maturity is up a few years. I take care of myself. My father helps. My father and I are very close now that he's sober in the past five years. The past five years we've become really, really close. It feels good. But he's in the position where I can't live with him because he lives with four other guys and he only has one room. So I can't live with him and he doesn't have any extra money. He never remarried but he has a girlfriend. I like her. This is the same one that he had the affair with. And at first I hated her. But after I got over that it was OK. And that's another thing. Like I said in the beginning, I hated my mother, I hated Mark, my mother's boyfriend, I hated my father, I hated Debby, his girlfriend, and I used to say "Well Debbie and Mark should get together so I can have my parents back." I was all alone. I still feel pretty alone, except for my dad.

Living in this place isn't so bad. I'm at the point now where I love it. Well, this sounds really odd, but now I have a sense of security. You know, I've grown very close to just about all the girls here, all the mothers. I'm not that close to Kathleen, because she just moved in or to Meredith, because she just moved in. And I'm in love with all the kids. One baby here, the first time she crawled I was in tears because I've known her ever since she was three months old and she's my little baby. I'm really attached to the kids here. I'm looking forward to leaving, but I know I'm going to miss everybody. We're already making all these plans and one of them, Laura, who is Janet's mother, has just gotten a nice house, with five bedrooms. She's going to be moving in. It has three bathrooms, and is just a huge house. So all the mothers are going to go over there and have a slumber party and I'm going to watch all the kids. So a part of me wouldn't mind staying here at the shelter for a while. The hardest part about living here is that my mother's very passive and me and the other women are not. And I take her place in like the adult role, because all of us women here are very strong-willed and we all have our own opinions and we all always voice them and my mother's like "Whatever, whatever." She's the peacemaker. And everybody here is more or less very strong-willed and really opinionated and I'm the same way. So I get upset a lot of times. We have spats. Someone's always fighting with someone. I hate the noise. I cannot stand it when I go to bed at night. It takes me an hour to get to sleep because everybody's down here laughing and playing cards doing whatever. The noise drives me up the wall. So I'm upstairs lying in bed and I'm going to kill everybody tomorrow. I'm going to kill everybody! I'm going to be such a bitch tomorrow.

And another thing that's hard is going to school from the shelter. For all my friends know, I just live in Eastover. They didn't know that I lived in a shelter. I never told them. At the beginning of the school year, I told two more people. Now only five of my friends know that I'm here. They don't really care. I'm pretty popular at school. That's why I wouldn't tell people I live in a shelter. I was really afraid that they'd judge me being homeless! They'd be thinking that I don't have a home and live in a shelter! In a way I know they wouldn't care. I wasn't worried about their opinions, but I was worried about it leaking out and other kids finding out. Other kids would think bad of me because people think being homeless is terrible. They think you have no money and the thing that goes with being homeless is that either you're drugged up like you're a major addict, or that your parents are druggies and that you're worthless. It's like this big chain. So that was the reason I didn't want it to leak out, that kids who weren't really my friends would find out. Some of my closer friends have been here, like my friend Rick. I've known him for eight years, so he knows everything about my family. He knows about the affair, he knows about my father having alcoholic problems, about Mark. He knows everything so coming to the shelter for him didn't matter. He's just a good friend. He's my other half. He's in twelfth grade. He used to live two streets away from the house I lived in. So he's been to all my birthday parties. He celebrated every Thanksgiving with us, exchanged Christmas gifts. I'm closer to him than I am my older sister. He's my protector.

When I get out of high school, I want to be a psychologist or something in that field or a counselor. Hopefully I'm going to college. My grades in school are all right, but they've been better. Last year, I got into deep depressions. I never got hospitalized. I'm sure a couple times I probably should have been though. I get really, really down. Really, really low. I think about just ending it all all the time. I've never tried it. I've never been that stupid. I see it as stupidity. I used to have really, really sick thoughts. Just last year I was always thinking about suicide, always. I see a counselor for that now. So last year my grades slipped. I've always been a high honor roll student, straight A's or every now and then a B. Last year everything went down. I was like getting just B's and C's which really wasn't all that bad, but it was worse than I'm used to. And my first quarter of school just ended last week. It was kind of hard, well no, it wasn't even hard, it's just that I wasn't really trying. I just went to school.

I'm getting in the habit of going to school every day again. I hadn't missed that much school. I've only missed five days. That's not a lot, but last year I missed like a month. I was always playing hookey and stuff, because I was upset. I didn't want to put up with anybody. I hated all my teachers. I hated walking the halls, I hated sitting there, learning. It was like "Ah!" I haven't had too much counseling. But I've been in Al-Ateen for four years. It's kept me alive. I have a pretty good concept of what's going on. I talk to my dad about my feelings. I can tell him how I feel and he won't get upset. Well, at times he does. It depends on what it's about. But he always tries to have an open mind, which is hard for him because it's hard for me to. And I'm exactly like my father. Exactly. I mean, I'm very strong-willed and I'm very stubborn.

But, I also like being cut off from everything. I like hibernating in my room and doing whatever. That's something I found really hard here, lack of privacy. And my mother and I really don't get along all that wonderfully and I have to share a room with her. I was like "Oh my God." That's something hard. But I also like being with other people and with all my friends. I'm the shoulder that everybody cries on. Everybody comes to me and I love it. I cry on my friend Rick's shoulder. He's really helped me a lot. And my other good friend, Cici, because her parents are both in the program. And I lived with her for three months.

I had seen this place from the outside of it many times. I grew up in this neighborhood. I'd seen it from the outside. I didn't expect it would be anything like this, though. I was expecting it to be kind of a little run-down. I expected it to have more bedrooms for some reason. I expected it to be more like a hotel than a house. I was really surprised, I was like, "A library, wow, there's furniture, wow." This is the model shelter.

COMMENTARY

Haydn recounts many losses: his mother to drugs, his home on several occasions, his stepfamily, and his friends. Similarly, Georgia has experienced many losses: her home, her childhood, her father to alcohol, and her mother to depression and to her boyfriend. Both Haydn and Georgia are sad and disappointed. They feel let down by those who cared for them. They are also angry, even though they express this in quite different ways. Georgia is very direct and talks to many people about her feelings. Haydn tends to keep it to himself and shares his feelings with only a select few. These feelings of sadness, disappointment, and anger are common in the stories of other homeless children.

Sadness is a predominant theme. Homeless children have endured multiple losses, which often leaves them feeling empty, sad, and depressed. Many are additionally burdened by recognizing and empathizing with the sadness their parents feel about the losses in their lives. A major loss for all of these children has been the loss of their home. This major loss has resulted in the loss of many if not most of the things and people in their lives to which they were most attached: personal belongings, extended family members, friends, their TV, their bedroom, and their neighborhood. The loss of privacy, a consequence of group living in a shelter, is particularly difficult for older school-age children and adolescents.

For many children, their feelings of sadness are often coupled with feelings of disappointment in their caretakers. Some of their stories reveal a sense of having been let down by their parents or other adults, whom they perceive as not having prevented the homelessness. For some, particularly adolescents, disappointment may turn to anger as they struggle to understand how homelessness happened to them.

Feelings of Sadness

The sadness that children feel about the plight they are in emerges repeatedly in the stories children tell about their life before and since entering the shelter. Some children express the sadness indirectly—for example, in the way that they describe the animals that were lost to them when they had to move to the shelter. Many report that their animal died or that they had to leave it behind. The sadness they feel for themselves and their sense of personal vulnerability are concretized in their accounts of what happened to their animals. Gertie, age seven, described how her cat died in the shelter:

When we moved in the first motel, we couldn't stay there. Well, we couldn't have cats there and when I tried to find my little cat, he drownded in the water. He hates water. Cats hate water, and we went fishing in the pond, behind the motel and he went in the pond and a fish ate him. I didn't find him. He was dead when I found him. I cried and my sister was sad.

Similarly, Katie, who is four, tells how her "kitty" became homeless. As expected for a child her age, she had difficulty recounting the details and feelings related to her experience of becoming homeless. However, she was able to describe with clarity the story of her kitty's experience in going to what she perceived was a special shelter for cats, presumably the Animal Rescue League.

While the story has many confusing details, Katie manages to communicate her ambivalent feelings about shelters. She views shelters as safe places with toys, but as places that separate the inhabitants from the people who love them. Katie described the cat shelter:

> [It's] where all the kitties are and you move and you can't move with them when they're having a baby. In the shelter they've got a lot of toys there for the kitties. My kitty's still there. The kitty had to go in a safe place. But they don't get beds. They live in a big cage. We can't get Sniffles back. We can't. We can't move with him because the shelter's going to get mad. The other shelter where Sniffles is. I think Sniffles liked going to the shelter. But I think he missed us. But we can't come see him, say hi to him. . . . That's why we can't say hi to him because he'll think that my mother's going to pick him up. And she's really not. I didn't feel sad for Sniffles. Sniffles liked going to the shelter.

For Sam, the sadness and loss he experienced becoming homeless is concretized in his account of being separated from his dog.

> I had a dog for a long time before I came here. We had to give him to a friend because we couldn't bring him down here with us. The shelter says "No animals." And, even if we move out of here, we can't get him back because he likes the people he's with right now. And me and him were best friends. His name was Ralphy. I always still remember him. I just hope he remembers me.

What is critical to Sam is not so much the loss of a dog, but the loss of a relationship with someone he loved.

Loss of Possessions

For many children, the sadness they experience is evident in their accounts of all the losses that have resulted from their becoming homeless. They readily list all the "pieces of home" that are missing in the shelter. The loss of personal belongings is one of the most obvious and concrete sources of sadness. Children are quick to enumerate all of the belongings that have been lost to them, either temporarily or permanently. Household furnishings, toys, and clothes are the losses that are most keenly felt. Vicky thinks that during her stay in the shelter she'll be "kind of sad because I won't get all my stuff and my stuffed animals which I've got three bags full."

Younger children miss the toys that they could not bring to the shelter. Charlie, who just turned seven, moved nearly two thousand miles with his mother on a bus. He described the experience very clearly:

I had to leave some stuff behind, like my bike. It was too big for the bus. And I didn't bring my Ninja Turtle, my Master Splinter or my bike, because there weren't enough room for them. I brought all my clothes and my best jacket. I felt sad about my bike. Sometimes I cry. I tell my mom. She says, "Well you're going to have to live with it."

Tara described the impact of selling her family's furniture: "When I saw it being selled, I was sad because all these memories were getting selled. Like, the car, and the couch, the TV, the clothes, the dresser, the bed, everything, even my clothes. A lot of memories were in those things that got sold."

Fourteen-year-old April was concerned that "when we were moving, like my shorts and stuff upstairs in my room, I never got them. And there were a lot of cute short outfits. Now I only got a little bit of short outfits." She went on to describe the piecemeal fashion in which her family's possessions were distributed to others:

My older sister, she got the couch and stuff. My mother was almost done paying on the washing machine and dryer, she gave it back to them. And the stereo went to this lady, Winona, my mother's friend, until my mother got an apartment. But I guess she used to be on drugs, and she sold it. She said someone stole it, but you know she stole it. And my mother ain't got the stereo no more. One of the TVs went to Mattina and the bed went to my cousin Linda. But they're her beds now. My mother gave them to her. And she gave Mattina the TV. The big floor TV she gave to my older sister. When we get an apartment, my mother's going to buy all new furniture. It was sad, all our stuff.

Many children respond to these losses by trying to hold on to and guard a few treasured possessions. One ten-year-old, who had moved at least a dozen times, described how she kept what was most valuable to her in spite of losing almost everything:

We get money from yard sales. We sell everything we have there. But I didn't sell my dolls and stuff from when I was little. I still got some of them. I'm going to keep them no matter what. In Texas, when we were in the mobile home, my bedroom was full of dolls. That was the best place we lived. (Stephanie)

Some describe not only the loss of furniture, but also of certain rooms in their house, particularly their bedroom. Dana gave the loss of his bedroom the same prominence as the loss of his friends: "I want to live at my old house, that's where all my friends live, that's where I lived for four years. And I moved from there. And I miss my old room and I miss my friends."

Loss of Privacy

The losses that are experienced in the shelter are concretized for older children and adolescents in what they describe as a loss of privacy. For a significant number of children, particularly those who are older, the loss of privacy is a major problem in the shelter or motel. Juan stated:

Before I came I thought it would be crowded, very very crowded and I wasn't going to like it. I knew that my family was going to have one room. We all sleep in the same room. I have my own bed. Sleeping all in the same room, it's not good, because of privacy. You don't get as much privacy as if you had your own room.

In the shelters, most families are assigned to a single room in which all the family members store their belongings and sleep. In the motels and hotels, this single and usually small room also constitutes the living and eating space. In such circumstances, privacy is not easily attained.

For older school-aged children and adolescents, for whom personal privacy is an important requirement of their developmental stage, the lack of privacy is particularly difficult. Ian, a young adolescent, views sharing a room with his mother as "unnormal." Nine-year-old Isabella also reflected on the abnormality of the situation:

We all live in one room here. The bad part is that I have to be with my brother in the same room. It's that bad because I'm not used to him. I'm not used to being with my mother in the same room, my little sister in the same room, my brother in the same room. I don't mind if my mother's there, and my little sister, because they're girls. Even though they're girls I don't like it. And my brother because he's a boy and I'm a girl, and my mother's a girl, my sister's a girl. It's hard because we're used to being separate, my brother separate, my mother separate, my little sister separate. We have to get dressed under the covers. My mother dressing in the bathroom, my brother getting under the covers, my little sister just dressing up right there with nobody seeing her.

Lisa expressed similar concerns:

Well you don't get much privacy at all. And I mean, I feel like I need privacy. You get dressed in a little bathroom. You don't have a bedroom. Like I put on makeup and stuff and you don't have somewhere to put it on. You just sit all around. I don't know. Everybody has to use the bathroom at once. The sleeping arrangement, I sleep on the bottom part of the couch, and Sam sleeps on the top because it's like a fold away bed. I mean, I'm too close to him as far as I'm concerned. It's just too close to him. And if I want to talk to my boyfriend on the phone or something, it's like "Shhhh." You whisper.

She went on to describe how she copes with this situation:

We're all on each other's nerves because we're always here. We're in such a small space and we're always here. Well, I leave often. I just like to say "See you later." Me and my boyfriend go out. We just go out. You know, just leave, say "See you guys later." I take my brother out sometimes. That way he gets out too. I don't know, it just seems like everybody has a temper.

Loss of Personal Space

For adolescents, who are struggling with issues of autonomy, the lack of personal space is distressing. Sam detailed his frustrations and his response to this situation. He didn't like the way that we're all in one room and that I can't have no privacy, where I like to have my own privacy because I have pictures to hang up, and I have friends that want to come over and stuff like that. I like to have my own room, to have them come over. I want to be able to talk to my friends about problems I had at school or anything like that because my parents don't really understand. . . . Sometimes I get sad here. I guess, more mad than sad because people, they want their own privacy and it's just hard because they get mad and they say stuff. Like my sister wants her own privacy and she gets mad, because other people are in her way and she just don't want people to watch her sleep, when they wake up. And that's the whole reason why I want a house.

The lack of ownership of the space, even the little space that is the family's room, is heightened in some shelters where lack of adequate funding and staffing forces shelter directors to close the shelters from early morning to early evening. During daytime hours, families have to find a place to spend their time or in some cases go to another site for a day program. For the children, this means being unable to go "home" to their room in the shelter after school and being unable to remain there during the weekend days. Isabella reported that "after school we go to my mother's friend's house and then we come over here. On Saturdays and Sundays I go to my mother's friend's house. I don't like that much. I'm not used to being houses to houses, because I always been in my own house. It feels sad not to have my own house."

Loss of Relatives and Friends

Not only are children sad about the loss of their possessions, their privacy, and their space, they also are hurt by the loss of particular people in their lives from whom they became separated when they moved out of their home. The shelter is frequently some distance from their old neighborhood. Even if it is within driving distance, most of these families have no transportation. Consequently, they are prevented from being with extended family members or friends. Many children, such as Marcus, miss the presence of a grandparent. "I was sad when we were leaving my grandmother's. My grandmother comes here sometimes. She's sad. She says, 'It isn't good living here.' "

In some families, one or two family members, for example the father or an older sibling, are not living in the shelter with the family. Welfare agencies or individual shelters may have regulations about housing children over a certain age or about housing the mother's husband or boyfriend, who may or may not be the father of the children. In some cases, the family believes that it will get housing quicker if there is not an adult male in the family. In any case, the resulting separation adds to the sadness of the child, who often does not understand the reasons for the separation. Javier stated: "My father's not here. He lives with my aunt and they're living in a motel because there's not much space nowhere else. I don't know why he's not with us. I'd like it better if he was here. He comes a little bit every day."

Some children in the shelters have not only moved out of their neighborhood, but also out of the city or state where they had been living. The total lack of familiarity with their new surroundings leaves them feeling lost. "I didn't know nothing when I came to here. That it would be cold, that it would snow, where anything was or who the people were. It was really, really different" (Charlie).

Loss of New Friends

For some children, the sadness is intensified by the circumstances of the shelter. Having made friends with other children and families in the shelter, children find themselves in the position of losing those friends when permanent housing comes through for a particular family. Since these moves sometimes happen quickly, young children often don't have time to say good-bye. One young boy who lived in a motel puzzled his parents by suddenly resisting going to school. He later explained his behavior. He had returned from school one day to find one of his motel friends gone. He came to the conclusion that as long as he never left the motel to go to school, nobody could leave him again.

Expressing Feelings of Sadness

Some children in the shelter are able to express their feelings of sadness very directly. A few describe talking to their friends in the shelter about their feelings. Others report that they often cry about how sad they feel about being homeless and in a shelter. These children indicate that they cry privately, usually in bed at night. Stephanie, who is ten, says she never tells her parents how she feels, but "when I go to bed, I cry real quiet in the pillow. I don't want them to hear." Kendra revealed: "I get sad sometimes. I cry by myself. Nobody knows though. The saddest thing is when I move away from my friends or my friends move away."

Children are not only cognizant of their own sadness; many are also keenly aware of the sadness of their parents at having to live in a shelter. They easily identify the various ways in which they know that their mother or father is sad. Jose revealed that he knows when his mom is sad "from looking at her face." Juan recognized the parallel between his experience and that of his mother:

> Being here makes me sad but I don't cry. I feel sad about it by myself. Sometimes I talk to my mother about it. I tell her how sad I am. She says she knows I'm sad. She knows because she feels the same way. I don't know if she cries about it. If she does I never see her. I think she does though. I don't like to talk about this stuff too much.

Often children who sense their parent's sadness try to protect them by hiding how sad they feel as children. "I don't tell her. Being homeless and stuff, it's not her fault" (Eddie).

Others try to reach out to their parents and do something to lessen the sadness. Speaking about the new apartment he anticipates moving to, Sean said: "There's already furniture in the house, but all we need is one little couch. And we need a rocking chair because my mom might want to rock in a chair." Juan explained that he helps his mother "like if she would tell me to do something then I could do it just so she won't feel bad. I help her make decisions, like whether or not to buy something, furniture or something like that."

Feelings of Disappointment and Anger

While children, in one way or another, express sadness about being homeless, they also deal with some of their pain by expressing disappointment in the people who are closest to them. Some children perceive their parents or other relatives as somehow being responsible for their move into the shelter. Younger children are disappointed when they realize the adult figures in their lives are not omnipotent. They may express a general and often vague feeling that their parents did not have things together enough to prevent homelessness.

For many, as they get older, the disappointment turns to anger at their parents, family members, or even themselves for not making things work better for their family. Many children, particularly those who are in the pre-adolescent stage, appear quite clear about what would have prevented their becoming homeless. They believe that if their parent had done a certain thing or engaged in some particular activity, they would not find themselves in this predicament. "She should of not drank like that. If she kept going to that AAA thing, we wouldn't be in this place now" (Mack).

Barbara, who is sixteen, alternately blames and absolves her parents. Speaking of her mother, she stated:

> I wonder why she did everything she did. I guess I think it's because she has a lot of problems. I guess she has those problems because some people are ready to cope with things at younger ages. She just wasn't. Her and my father went through a lot of problems before they got married. Having no place to live, staying out on the streets, finding any way they could to survive. Because my father and mother were alcoholics and any money they got they just blew for alcohol. They were nineteen and twenty when they got married.

Sometimes adolescents believe that one parent is more competent than the other, and are angry at the competent parent for not saving them from homelessness. This is true for Dana, who enjoyed living with his father and stepmother in a home that provided for all of his needs. Dana came to the shelter at his father's request, to better his mother's chances for obtaining housing. Dana copes with the situation by repeatedly asserting that his father will come and take him back at a moment's notice.

Some children express intense anger, not so much at parents, but at more distant relatives, or even the shelter staff and guests. Bitter resentment is often expressed toward grandparents or other relatives for not opening their homes to them, or for asking them to leave after the strains of doubling up became too great. Other children express anger and hostility toward those associated with the shelter, as Tara did when she announced that all the people in the shelter "stink," that "the staff and the other people in this place are all rotten."

Although it is infrequent, a few adolescents express anger at themselves for getting into a predicament that resulted in their having to go to the shelter. For example, Kendra expressed deep regret for losing her foster placement: "I wish I hadn't messed up. I could be there now."

Some children's anger and disappointment reaches all the way to God. While Ian ultimately attributed his family's homelessness to a "messed up" mom, uncaring grandparents, and a system that "stinks," he eventually claimed that even the God he had come to know was indifferent to his plight: "I don't believe in God because it's so dumb, sitting there praying to a wall. He doesn't do nothing back. It's just dumb. I don't like God."

As they mature, adolescents come to realize that homelessness is the result of complex and interacting conditions and circumstances, and cannot be blamed on one or a few people. While they may, at times, point their anger in many directions, they ultimately become angry at life itself for having cheated them out of what they had assumed was everyone's right—a home.

Chapter Six

"I'm Always Scared":
Fear and Uncertainty

MARCUS

Marcus, age eight, and Sean, age six, whose story was presented earlier, have been living in the shelter with their mother and three-year-old sister for over two months. After moving from another large city, they lived a short time with the maternal grandmother in this current city. The move to the shelter was precipitated by a fight between the mother and the grandmother.

Now I'm seven, but I'm going to be eight in September. My brother's birthday is in August. I've been living here for a couple of months. I think it's not too good. . . .

Here's not like a house. The machines don't work. Like the sink. But the sink works at my old house. It's not clean here, but it's clean at your own house. Here has bugs and your own house doesn't. At your own house you can have your own back yard. You can play when you get ready. And I can go to bed when I want to. Here, on school nights you have to go to bed at nine o'clock. And here nobody ever does their chores. But I had chores at home, and at home you do your chores. Only my mother and another few people do their chores. Other people don't because if they have to clean up from somebody else, they won't do their chores. It's kind of hard living here. I don't like the beds. They're uncomfortable.

Before I came here I was living in New York. I got here by taking a bus. I didn't always live in New York. I was raised here and I went to New York. I was around five when I went to New York. I went to kindergarten there. And I went to first grade there. I went to second grade in New York and here. But I didn't just finish the second. I came back here and went to school, at Cheney, but I didn't finish a grade. I didn't graduate yet. I don't know why I didn't finish. I missed some school before I came here. Because we were getting ready to go to here to visit my grandmother. We left New York and came to here to visit my grandmother. When we came we lived at my grandmother's house. When I was there I went not to Cheney, but to another school. I was there with my grandmother for a couple of days. Then when I came to here, to the shelter, I came from my grandmother's house. We walked here. No we took a cab. We didn't stay at my grandmother's house because my mother and my grandmother had a fight and my mother had to leave. I knew we were going to a shelter. I thought it was going to be not pretty. I wasn't happy to come here. I said to my mother, "I don't want to go live in a shelter." Because I didn't want to live in a shelter with all other people I didn't know. And I thought it was going to look like all messed up, like with cracks and crayons drawn on the walls. I knew I had my own bedroom.

I didn't tell my friends. Because they'd all make fun of me. They'd say, "Marcus lives in a shelter." I don't know why they think it's bad. We couldn't get a regular apartment when we moved out of my grandmother's because my mother didn't have any money. I'm going to be here a couple of days and then we're getting ready to move. We haven't found one place yet. Not yet. I'm going to see some places. There's one on Francis Street. I hope they'll be good. I want to get out of here. When I get into my own house it will be better. Beds. I won't have to worry about noise, no bugs, no roaches, no mosquitos, no cracks, nobody telling me when to go to bed.

When I first came here I was scared. I'm scared of the strangers that I don't know. I thought they would be unkind people. If I asked them something they would say "No." I thought they'd cut me. The people who live here are noisy people. I don't know why they're here. Because maybe they had nowhere else to go. When my mother said we didn't have no place else to go, I was scared. I was sad when we were leaving my grandmother's. My grandmother comes here sometimes. She's sad. She says "It isn't good living here." She doesn't like the people. And there are bugs, bugs that are poison and fly around here.

Me and my brother live in a room. My mother's next door. My teacher doesn't know that I live in a shelter. No, but the secretary does. The secretary that types at school. She knows because she goes to a church across the street. I don't want her to know. Nobody else at school knows. Just Maggie. I don't know what the teachers would say.

My mom gets money from the bank. She can't get enough money for an apartment because she's saving up her money. She's saving it up to get, I don't know what. There's nothing good about living here. I just don't like it. When I grow up I'm going to have a job and take care of my mother and sister and my brother. And my kids and my wife. We're going to have a home. We'll get it because I'm going to work real hard. And get a car. I sometimes get sad for my mom now. I got sad when we had to move. And I was sad for my mom then too. I thought I was going to be taken away from her, by the foster people. They would take me because we live in a shelter. I told nobody I was worried. My mother knew. She said "Don't be afraid." I've never lived with foster people but I know about them because my mother told me. She said that if mothers or their fathers can't take care of their kids, they will go to a foster home. I thought because we came to a shelter they could say my mommy wasn't taking care of me. I don't worry about it anymore. Also before I came, I was worrying about people I don't know. They scared me and frightened me. Because I didn't know them. I didn't tell my mommy I was scared and frightened. She just knows. She says, "Don't be afraid Marcus, don't be afraid." I was crying when I came here.

TROY

Troy, eleven, and his sister April, fourteen, belong to a family of eleven girls and one boy. Only April, Troy, and their sixteen-year-old sister Karyn, who is pregnant, live with their mother in the shelter. The other children are older and living on their own. Their mother is drug-involved and the family was evicted from their lifelong home after their apartment was raided by the police. Troy did not join the family in the shelter immediately, but stayed with his aunt. Troy's father, who is not the father of the other children, lived with the family a short time after Troy was born. He has since left, but lives in the same area as the family, and pays child support. Troy's father has nine children from other relationships.

I'm eleven and in fifth grade, going to sixth. I went to school in Kenwood, Taylor School. I've been going there for a whole year. In fourth, I went to Foster School in Brenton. Same with third and second and always. I always lived in Brenton. Then I went to Kenwood because my mother had no place to live and my aunt just said that she'd take me and the school said it's okay. We were evicted onto the streets. Because these boys used to hang in front of my house and my mother kept calling and complaining and then they just kept getting fed up because every time the cops came, they would think that the boys ran into my house. So they just evicted my mother, because these boys were drug dealers. But they never came in my house. They just hung in front of my house. Because we live near the woods and maybe they think if the cops come they can run into the woods. I knew one of those boys.

I didn't really care when I found out we had to move, because I wanted to move. I really didn't like that street, because I didn't have anything to do. I had lots of friends. But if you were sitting on the porch in the front of your house and the cops come and they drive by then they'll tell you to get in your house. Like if you're sitting on your porch and it's ten o'clock and you're just sitting there talking with your friends then they'll just tell you to get in your house. I don't know why. My mom was moving before they evicted her. When she heard that they would evict her, she just started giving up and wanted to try to come here. And we were talking to Claire and my mother and my sister, Elizabeth. And then my mother came in here. She wanted to come here because she said it would help her get a house or apartment or something. Someplace to live. I don't know why she couldn't just get one herself. I was kind of happy we came to Kenwood. I was going to be going to school at my aunt's. I liked living there. But I wanted to come back here to Brenton, too, so I could come back to school in Brenton. I liked school in Kenwood but I didn't have that many friends. I only had Andy and I used to hang around with his friends and they were kind of little.

It's more peaceful in Kenwood. Because there are really no cops coming around. Late at night, when you're up, you hear the cars burning rubber and stuff. Around here cars come speeding up the corner. My old street wasn't that peaceful. Cops used to tell you to get in your house and stuff and you're just standing out there relaxing, getting some air or something. They would tell you to get in your house. Then I really didn't have nothing to do. People shooting off guns and stuff. I'm glad I'm not there at my old street. I think the place I might go to will be better. I don't know how I know. I just think it. I think it will have security guards riding around patrolling the area and stuff and a pool, like where anybody can go. . . .

But I kind of like living here. It's safe. You don't have to worry about anybody robbing you. I had those worries in my old place. Nobody ever robbed me, but I worry about it. Here, they always have someone watching the front door, whenever somebody comes in they can't get upstairs. I also like that here you can have animals like they have a house cat and a house dog. On my old street you couldn't have no animals. If I could pick an animal I would pick a dog. Here, there is Humphrey the dog. I like Humphrey.

It's also good here, like if you need hair spray or deodorant or something or a toothbrush you can just ask one of the workers to get you one, and if you didn't live in the shelter you have to go buy your own. Here you have a curfew. You have to be in by a certain time. And if you lived in your own house you won't have to come in a certain time, you can come in anytime you want to. A curfew here is good, because kids aren't supposed to be out past eleven o'clock or they could get hurt. Because somebody could ride by and shoot them, like somebody speeding or something and they might get hit or something.

A worker comes to wash the place everyday. And, they donate food to you and stuff. It's sort of like if you buy your own food or your own clothes, they still donate clothes to you and donate food to you. It's good because if you need food and you had to go shopping, a donation comes and then you can sit down and eat before you go shopping or something. And if there's enough food then you don't have to go shopping. I never ran out of food at my old house. My mom got money from my father. Right now my dad's at work. He lived in our old house with us. Now he lives on the North Side. I don't know why we're not living with him. I guess because my momma just wanted to come to the shelter. So we came here. She can get her own apartment. My dad's living by himself. He's the dad just for me, not my sisters. But like he still gives my other sisters money and stuff. And he has nine other kids of his own. I don't know all of them. I just remember I have two other sisters and I know three of my other brothers. All together I have twenty-one brothers and sisters. I sometimes can't remember their names. One time I was with my sister in town and I started calling her Stacey for some reason. That wasn't her name. My sister that was with her, I started calling her Mattina. It was getting all mixed up. These were my mother's kids. With my father's kids I'm not the youngest. I'm older than one of my sisters. Having that bunch of kids, I think it's crazy. It's too many kids, because you have to pay child support. You pay the child 'til they can get out on their own. My dad pays child support. He pays just for me and one of my brothers and one of my sisters. He has a lot of money left because he puts money in the bank.

Some things I like about living here. The people treat you nice and we take long trips and stuff. If people have something they offer it to you and you don't have to ask them. Some people just sit there and eat it right in your face. Some people in here will ask you if you want some of it. Staff and the people that live here, they're all nice. There's nobody I don't like. There's nothing about living here I don't like. But I'd rather live in my own house. You can have company over any time you want to. In the shelter, say I told my brother Rob to come over, company has to leave at eleven o'clock unless they're going to spend the night. And in a house you can have your house the way you want it too. If you come here you have to do a certain chore, but at your own house you can do whatever chore you pick. Here they don't want the shelter to be dirty, but if you want your own house to be dirty you can have it dirty. If you live in a shelter you have to have it clean. I don't get chores here, though. I guess they don't give them to kids. . . .

People are here because they're homeless. That means they got no place to live. If they get evicted or are kicked out of their house, they have to sleep house-to-house or in their car or something. You cou. j get killed by people in your car. Somebody could be running by and catch you and just decide to kill you. It's kind of like if a killer is running by and he killed somebody else in his house and he'd try to kill you, too. Some people here got evicted and stuff and can't go to another apartment because they can't find it too fast. Because some apartments are in bad neighborhoods and you want to move into good neighborhoods that are big enough for your family. . . .

I didn't tell my teacher I lived here. I just wanted to keep it to myself. Kids keep it to themselves because somebody else might hear them, tell another person. Like I tell somebody and they tell somebody else and it keeps going around and around the school. What would happen is that if a person I told tells some other person, I might try to beat that person up. For telling. . . .

I was living with my aunt before I come with my mother. Me and my cousins were standing around. My aunt asked my mother if she wanted me to come stay with her until the whole year of school. Since she couldn't find a place to live, my mother said yes. That was a good idea. But I missed my mom a little bit. She came to see me every weekend. . . . I didn't ever find out why my mom doesn't have enough money. She gets her money from welfare I know. But I don't know how much. I get allowance. . . . I wish a lot that we would get a nice house.

COMMENTARY

Children who become homeless have many reasons for being afraid. The assault that homelessness makes on their sense of security leaves them fragile and vulnerable. Marcus and Troy express many fears. Marcus is particularly worried that coming to the shelter means he will be taken away from his mother. Troy, who has lived in a world with considerable violence, fears for the safety of himself and his possessions.

In general, children who are homeless express a number of fears about what may happen to them, both in the shelter and after leaving the shelter. These fears center around three domains: first, their initial worries just prior to and immediately upon arrival at the shelter about what will happen to them in the shelter and about how the shelter will treat children; second, their ongoing fears while in the shelter about the ability of the shelter to keep both them and their family safe; and third, their fears about the future and life after the shelter, a fear exacerbated by the uncertainty of when they can move out.

Fear about Coming to the Shelter

Prior to coming to the shelter and in the early days after their arrival, many younger children are afraid that the breakup and loss of their home implies the breakup and loss of their family. This is particularly true for children who have had any prior experience with children's protective services, or have heard of or known children who have been removed from their family of origin. Not a few children in homeless families report being frightened that when they came to the shelter, they would be taken away by "foster people." Bethany, age twelve, was reluctant to come to the shelter because "my brother says that we would get tooken away and stuff like that. I don't know why."

Some of these fears reflect not only the child's earlier experiences, but also their level of cognitive development. Young children's prelogical reasoning often leads to fears that are unrealistic from an adult's perspective. Children sometimes put two unrelated ideas or events together on the basis of some superficial similarity between the ideas or events. Such reasoning led Marcus to worry unnecessarily. It was his understanding that children were taken away from parents who couldn't take care of them. It was also his understanding that going to a shelter meant that parents couldn't take care of their children. Consequently, he concluded that children who went to a shelter would automatically be taken away from their parents. "I thought because we came to the shelter they could say my mommy wasn't taking care of me."

Some children not only fuse the breakup of their home with that of their family, they also link it with harm or destruction to themselves, to their own person. Children worry that there will be "bad people" in the shelter who will hurt them or find a way to "get them." As Jose explained: "People that I didn't know made me scared. I thought they would be bad, like, strange people, who just want you to try to be friends and they would get me and stuff."

The sense of fear and anxiety that children have about what the shelter will be like is often expressed not in specific concerns but rather in a vague and general sense of impending doom. Imagining a place to live that is not a home—a non-home—is impossible for many younger children, particularly if they have been given no concrete details. It is this sense that Sean expressed when he described being afraid because "I thought I was moving to nowhere." Children who have been prepared for the event by receiving a description of the shelter from their mothers appear to worry less about their safety. However, oftentimes the mothers are themselves uncertain about what it will be like and are unable to give the child this information. Children sense their mother's concerns, adding to their own anxiety.

Fear of Being Put Out

There are many aspects of shelter living that create worry and anxiety for children after they arrive at the shelter. The most universal fear of children in the shelter and motels is that they will be "thrown out" and have nowhere to go. Many imagine themselves living on the sidewalk. It is a fear that has lived inside many of them for a long time, even prior to coming to the shelter. Ingrid described her worries this way: "Sometimes when you're poor you can't pay the bills. If you don't pay the bills and stuff, you'll have to move out or something and you might live on the street." She later elaborated on this fear and its source: "Once on a commercial I saw a lady and she had two children, a baby and about a four-year-old, and they were just sitting on a street crying. They were crying because they didn't have any food or anything and they were starving. Sometimes I have bad dreams about it."

This fear is particularly apparent in children who have little or no information about, or only a vague understanding of, how their family lost their home and how they happened to find themselves in a shelter. In addition, their lack of awareness of how the welfare process works leads them to worry about the stability of the shelter and about the steps involved in their receiving another home. This fear is often compounded by their parent's confusion about how the system works.

The difficulty experienced by parents and staff in comprehending the often overwhelming complexities of welfare regulations is reflected in their inability to explain present and future events to the children in simple terms. Often children pick up bits and pieces of explanations, but because they cannot integrate them into a cohesive account, they are not reassured. "We're waiting for a certificate or paper or something. It's coming from some lady somewhere. My mother said she doesn't know when it's coming, that we just have to wait" (Raphael).

Children are most certain of the requirement that they must wait. Waiting is perceived by children as the single activity they can engage in that will get them a home. This passive response adds considerable frustration and anxiety to their day-to-day lives. During the waiting, children begin to worry that something will go wrong resulting in their being put out of the shelter. To the children, breaking the rules is what is most likely to go wrong.

Each shelter or motel has its own set of expectations or rules for shelter residents. The clarity, detail, and number of these rules varies from shelter to shelter. In some shelters, consequences for violations of the rules are also clearly articulated, with eviction as the ultimate consequence for serious or repeated violations. In shelters where the rules are a significant concern, and in which there is a limit to the number of violations, children are often terrified that their family will be thrown out when they, or even more critically, when their parents break a rule.

Jose, for example, described how his infraction occurred when he came back to the shelter late due to a baseball practice the staff did not know about. Although concerned about his own warning, Jose seems more troubled by the fact that his mother got a warning. "I don't know for what. I wish I did. I was at school when she had a warning. I didn't ask her what it was for. She got sad." He went on to say that because of such incidents "I'm afraid we'll get thrown out." Likewise, Gertie, who is seven, explained that her "father's friends come here and they don't live here so they can't come here. Like he said if they come one more time we might get kicked out. I don't know where we'll go."

Many children recall how they unwittingly broke a rule, and the fright that followed. Young children, in particular, do not have the cognitive and moral maturity to distinguish between major and minor infractions. They do not realize that getting thrown out is probably not as easy to

accomplish as it seems. The state of constant tension this situation creates
was detailed by nine-year-old Tucker:

> Sometimes you have to pass the rooms of other people at night when
> I have to go to bed and I'm always scared that I'm going to wake
> up somebody! Yeah. And I don't like waking up people. It scares
> me, like someone's going to do something if I wake them up. Like
> tell something. Something like that. Something might happen. I
> don't know. I'm always scared. . . . I'm scared I'm going to do
> something wrong, and I don't know that it's wrong and I'm going
> to get in trouble for it. My whole family's going to get kicked out
> or something like that.

Children are also afraid of lesser consequences of rule violation.
Four-year-old Daniel's normal childhood fear of ghosts is compounded
in shelter living. He tells of how, scared in his sleep about ghosts, he has
to search through the shelter to find his mother. More than his fear of
the ghosts, Daniel is afraid "that all the people are going to get mad at
me if I go down those stairs to find her. Them downstairs will get mad."
Children in shelters also are worried about their personal safety.
Because the barriers to both the inside of the building and to each family's
space are more permeable than they are in a house or apartment, and
because of the unfamiliar nature of the shelter and its inhabitants, children
often feel very vulnerable. They fear that people or events inside the
dwelling might harm them. Tucker reports how afraid he and his sister
were at breakfast when a "strange-looking man who lives here too, he
wouldn't speak to us when we said hello. He just stared at us. He was
weird like. It made us scared."

Fear of Being Hurt

Some fear that people from the outside might hurt them by breaking
in or by destroying the shelter. A number of eight-year-old Vicky's
worries fall into this category:

> I worry about stuff living here. Like fires. And drinking. And
> getting kicked out. I worry about fires because then we won't be
> able to get our stuff and we'll lose our stuff and maybe we won't be
> able to get it back and I've got my favorite stuffed animals there.
> I'll just grab them with me. And run out. I think there might be
> fires because if someone like pours gasoline around here and then

someone, like the cars leaving gasoline dripping and people like throw down their cigarettes or forget to stomp them out. Because that'll be a huge fire. . . . I worry about break-ins. They could just hop over the fences because it's not too big and then they could just slip something in the screen and come in. And I worry about getting kicked out. Because if you break too many rules you get a notice and you get kicked out if you do break any more and then you'll have to work on housing and stuff like that alone. If we got kicked out we wouldn't have a big chance of getting welfare, because we won't have anyone to help us.

While children sometimes see the shelter as a place in which they might get hurt, many perceive it as a safe place. From their perspective, it may not be the safest of all places, but it seems safer than what they knew. In many ways, it serves as a haven from the violence they had known. Often their previous home was in an inner-city area that was riddled with gangs and violence. For some, even the boundaries of their own apartment could be penetrated by people whom they perceived to be a threat. Break-ins were not uncommon in their neighborhoods. Some children report being frightened by friends or acquaintances of their parents. Others detail the frightening presence of drugs or weapons in their homes. Some children clearly see the shelter as a better alternative. For children like Troy, life before the shelter was unsafe and frightening. The shelter protects him.

Some children express gratitude that the shelter provides for them so that their mother does not have to work. Having been exposed to violence, in their own families or in the neighborhood, they worry about being harmed if their mom leaves them in someone else's hands. If they had an apartment of their own, then their mother might have to leave and go to work. Living in the shelter spares them this worry, enabling the mother to stay home and protect them.

Fear about the Future

Perhaps the most overwhelming anxiety for children is related to their future. The immediate worry about getting a house preoccupies most families in the shelter. Children are very aware of their parents' and the staff's efforts to find a place for them to live. This activity stimulates their fears of what will happen to them when they leave. For many, the situation they know, as bad as it may be, is better than the situation they don't know. Raphael, who is seven, was adamant about his fears of life outside the shelter. "This place—it's not good. . . . There's bad people that hit kids and take kids too. They're out there, everywhere, where the houses are going to be."

Children are worried about where they will be living, the kind of house, the neighborhood, the location. They are uncertain about where they will move to after the shelter. They have no idea even in which city or town they will be living, and worry about how far away it will be from friends and family. Ryan, who is twelve and had moved from out of state, had little information. "We'll be at the shelter for a while, probably for the rest of the year, I don't know. We're going to move. I don't know when. I don't know where we're moving to. I guess wherever they put us. There's a place I want to move to. I don't know the name of it."

Others worry about the type of neighborhood in which their new house will be located. Twelve-year-old Bethany is less than enthusiastic about her family's potential move from the shelter. When thinking of a new home, she asks herself, "what if it's a bad place or something. What if there's shooting, fighting." Prior to moving into the shelter, most of these children have been living in unsafe neighborhoods. Street crime and violence are vivid and recent memories for them. They fear the same when they finally "get a house." While they may hope for the best, they have good reason to expect the worst.

Similarly, they worry about the condition of the house they will move into. Many remember very clearly the dismal conditions inside their former homes. They report bugs, roaches, broken windows, non-working stoves, leaking roofs, lead paint, peeling ceilings, and holes in the walls. The shelter may not be the lap of luxury, but it frequently is an improvement on the physical living conditions they have known. Their desperate desire for their own home does not relieve their apprehension about what this home will be like.

Not only do the children in the shelters not know where they will eventually be living, they also do not know when the move will be taking place. This uncertainty leaves them worried about making new friends. Is it worth it or will their family be gone soon? "I'm not sure what to do. I like her but I don't want to get too much friends with her because maybe there's no time. We'll be moving again. I don't know when" (Lisa).

While children are uncertain about the "when and where" of their eventual move, the uncertainty that gives rise to most of their fears is the "how" of the move, the process by which they will be able to secure a permanent home. Very young children have little or no idea of the process involved, and often think it is just a matter of finding an available place. However, even young children quickly begin to realize that the enterprise involves money. They understand that getting a house is related to their mother's having money. But how exactly Mom gets money is a mystery to many of the younger children, and this vagueness intensifies their anxiety. They report bits and pieces of a story, such as "she gets it from my uncle, she gets money from welfare, but we have no money," but they are unable to specify precisely how or when she will get money or why it is she does not have enough money. They do not perceive it as an orderly process that follows some rules. In many cases, this limited cognitive understanding may be reinforced by the reality of the family's situation, in which money is only irregularly available, even for necessities. Unable logically to understand the process, children feel no sense of control over what is seen as the crucial factor in getting a house—that is, sufficient money.

School-age children, on the other hand, are aware that their mother has a steady source of income, like the monthly check, but their limited understanding of math prevents them from realizing that the fixed amount of the check must be used to cover all expenses, and not simply housing. They assume initially that if their mother has any money, they can have a house. However, this assumption is soon tempered by the realization that their mother's money must be used to pay for all their needs, not just housing. They remember that when living at home, they had sometimes run out of money for food and bills, and were worried that they would not have enough. Even though they would like more money for toys or clothes, their greatest fear is running out of money for food and rent.

Most children's explanation for why there is not enough money is simply that their mother does not get enough. Some suggest that if she could work it would get her more money, but that she cannot work because she is unable to find a job or someone to mind the children. Children at this age begin to sense, but do not articulate explicitly, the catch-22 quality of their mother's life. Many children feel helpless to help their mother because they are "too little to work." Some attempt to give her some relief by small donations. Sean had told a friend that he lived in the shelter because "we didn't have enough for the bills from my house." His friend J. J., who was living at the shelter because his house had burned down, subsequently "saved up some money and he gave it to me, but he didn't make that much. It wasn't enough money."

With more cognitive maturity, adolescents understand the process that is involved in securing a new place to live. They realize that getting an apartment requires money, and that maintaining an apartment requires not only a continuous source of money, but also the ability to manage money effectively. They understand that they are in a shelter because of a failure of the family's resources, primarily its finances. However, many believe that their parents were unable to manage for other reasons, such as not working or being involved with alcohol or drugs. They worry about whether things will be different when they get new housing. Their overriding fear about the future is that their family will not make it when they are on their own again. Their experience has taught them a bitter lesson about their family's frugality and vulnerability. They are aware that what happened before could happen again, and wonder if their family will manage to survive on the "outside."

"I've Seen and I Know What I've Seen": Violence and Substance Abuse

KENDRA

Kendra, who is seventeen, lives in the shelter with her father and twelve-year-old brother. She has six stepsiblings, four of whom are her father's children and two of whom are her mother's children. She initially lived with her mother, but left to join her father and paternal grandmother. After many moves, they ended up in a motel and subsequently this shelter, where they have been for three weeks. Her mother is an active alcoholic and her father is a recovering alcoholic. Her mother is currently engaged in a custody battle over her two other children, with the threat that they will be taken by the state protective services unit. Kendra herself has been in several foster homes.

I think living here is alright. Me, my brother Matthew, who's going to be thirteen, and my dad are here. We've been here a week. Before this, we were at the Westside Motel in Seton. We were there about a month. Before that we were at my grandmother's. Me and dad stayed at my grandmother's. My brother just moved in with us like a month ago. I've been with my dad for almost four months. Before that I was living with my mother, in Seton. Then I went to stay with my dad at my grandmother's and Matthew was still living with my mother. Now he just came to live with me and my dad. I moved from my mom's because she was drinking too much. My dad just got out of rehab and my mom was drinking too much so I just didn't live there anymore, because we fought and argued too much. The arguing got really big for her. My dad was in rehab, so that's gotten better. He doesn't drink as much. But he wasn't drinking for two whole months straight. And then, he lost custody of my other two little sisters and he just started drinking again. So I don't know. It's pretty scary for me. But he's not as bad as my mother when she's drinking. She gets all out of hand and goes crazy and stuff like that. He don't. She doesn't hurt us when she's drinking. But she just calls me all kinds of names and stuff. She's going to AA now. I saw her the other day. Because, I have another baby sister, she's two, and the courts are going to take her away. They gave her three months to straighten out and get her life together. She doesn't want to lose her so I guess that's what she's going to do. She's going to just try to straighten out.

My dad lost custody of the other two kids because he didn't live with their mother. But now him and my stepmother are getting married. So they're getting along better now. He sees the kids everyday. So that feels better. This has been going on since I was little. My parents both used to drink. I was nine when they split up. They were drinking before that. They used to fight a lot. Hitting fights. I cried and told my dad to stop and stuff like that. He doesn't really hit. He doesn't hit my stepmother or nothing. They get along good. I was scared because I didn't want him to hurt my mother. They get along better now that they're not married than when they were. I'm the oldest in the family. I helped bring up Maurice. I always used to babysit and stuff. My little baby sister, I always used to watch her and stuff. I know how to do all the jobs. I should, because I had four little brothers and sisters. My grandmother, my mother's mother, took care of me. I used to live with her for a while. She spoiled me. She used to buy me anything I wanted and take me out places. Because I was a girl, that's why I got spoiled the most. The person I get along with most is my Aunt Ann Marie's best friend. For the past couple months, she's helped me out a lot. She's always been there for me. I get along with her the best out of everybody. She's always there when I'm crying or I'm upset and stuff like that. She's always there for me. And she's moving away in August to California. She said as soon as I get out of school I could go live out there. I really like her. She just started coming like when her baby was like two or three months. She always used to come over my grandmother's when I was there. Then I used to babysit for her. Then I really got to know her. She's really cool. She's like a big sister I never had. It feels good because she's just always there for me when I need to talk to her. When I'm upset, she's there.

I get most upset sometimes when my dad drinks. I get sick of it. I just get mad and I tell him. He says, "I'm an alcoholic" and stuff like that. "I know I gotta straighten out" but he doesn't seem to. He's always here, though, for us. We're always fed and clean so it doesn't really matter. Well, it matters a little. But I'm trying to do my best. . . .

I've moved a lot in my life. I've been in four or five different schools. All I know is I'm not going to a different school next year. I don't care if I'm out here or not, I'll drive to school if I'm here, because I don't want to go to a different school. I want to be with my friends my last year of high school. I don't like all this moving. The worst part is having to go to different schools and meeting new friends. I don't like that. Having no friends. I get mad about it and when I do I get mad at my mom because she always moves. She just gets sick of living in one place. She's like a gypsy.

I've been in foster homes. In the last one I was in, it was my decision to go. I shouldn't have messed up. I could have still been there now. I still talk to the people. I had to leave because I got in an argument with one of the kids that was living there and then I got in an argument with the mother. But I did like it there. They were nice people. They were always there, and I had older sisters and brothers to look up to. I was there two years. I chose to go there. I still call them. They don't call me. There's no phone here. I saw them a couple months ago. I saw them last vacation. I went over their house. She was shocked to see me. I just showed up. She was happy to see me. I wished I hadn't messed up. I could be there now. Before that I was in a foster home in fourth grade. And I ran away because the lady used to beat us. I ran, and I called my grandmother and she came and picked me up. I had to go to the foster home in the first place because my mother and my grandmother and my father were fighting over me and my brother. They all wanted custody and so they just thought it would be best for us to go into a foster home. So me and my brother went. And I ran. She used to beat me and my brother. My brother stayed there and they went and got him. People believed us. My grandmother didn't like them anyway. Then I went back to live with my grandmother. I don't know why they were fighting over custody in the first place.

Living in this place, at Harbor House, it's alright, for a while. There's just no kids my age. All day I watch TV in my room. At night I go to Oak Street and call my friends. We meet. They don't know I'm here. I don't tell them. It's embarrassing. Living in a shelter's embarrassing. Everybody knows that you're poor. I'm not poor but, still, I'm homeless and everybody will know that. They wouldn't disown me. It's just embarrassing for me. If they say "Where do you live?" I say, "Oh I live

down that street over there." Well my best friend, she knows where I
live. She doesn't say anything. The hardest part for me is not having a
phone. There are pay phones, but it costs so much. It's hard. I can't talk
to my friends. So I call them up, from here or Oak Street. Some of them
live in Westfield, and I try calling them. If not, I just go down there with
my little brother, meet up with people. We can stay out at night 'til eleven
o'clock on Sunday to Thursday and twelve on Friday and one on Saturday.
At night my dad goes over his girlfriend's. He doesn't drink every day.
He's been sick, so he hasn't been drinking. Just sometimes. But he can't
work because he's got back and head injury. He got beat up by two kids.
He got hit in the back with a jack and hit over the head like four or five
times with an axe handle. That was a couple of years ago. One's in jail
for murder, for life.

I would rather be in my own house because I'd feel better living in my
own house than living here, because then my friends would know that I
had a house. They wouldn't think I was living here. The other people here
are pretty nice. They're here because they're homeless too. Maybe they
got kicked out of the house they were living in before. And they're poor
and they don't have money. Some people live in a shelter because there's
not a lot of houses. And money, the state doesn't have a lot of money. We're
trying to get a certificate now to get a house. I want it to be in Seton or
Bronville. My dad wants it in Westfield. He'll probably win. . . .

The hard thing for kids living in places like this is that there's not that
much to do. It's boring. They don't have a swimming pool, they don't
have nothing. They're just here all day. It's especially boring when you're
seventeen. All day I just watch TV and walk around and stuff. I talk to
my cousin, because she lives in here, too. She's in her twenties.

DANA

*Dana, who is fourteen, came to the shelter with his brother Haydn
whose story we heard earlier. Their mother, who is with them in the
shelter, had been incarcerated on drug-related charges. The boys
have been living with their father and stepmother. They are now
back with their mother who has just been released from prison and
are waiting in the shelter for permanent housing.*

Before here, me and my brother had been living with my father in
Fairhale. We're here because I guess we'd been living with my father so
long my mother missed us. I mean she wanted us to come live with her.
But all my friends are back in Fairhale. I want to go back there. I've

been here a week. . . . When I lived with my father and stepmother, we had seven bedrooms, a family room, a rec room, a place where you have a jacuzzi room in it, we had two bathrooms and we had a master bedroom and a big backyard. I have five stepbrothers and a stepsister. My stepmother works three jobs. And my father works two. My step-grand-mother comes over every Tuesday to watch the kids. She helps clean and stuff. She cooks like for the whole week. . . .

I wasn't happy about coming. I did it because my mother made me. I don't know why, I guess she wanted us to live with her. I want to live at my old house, that's where all my friends live, that's where I lived for four years. And I moved from there. And I miss my old room and I miss my friends and every time I could stay out. I'm fourteen now. I was at that house for about four years. Before I moved to Fairhale I lived in Maine with my aunt. And then I moved back to my grandmother's, then from my grandmother's I moved back to Fairhale, and from Fairhale I moved here. Also, when I was like seven, I lived in Riverside. Kinder-garten I lived at my grandmother's. Then in fourth grade I went to live in Maine with my aunt. . . .

I went to live in Fairhale with my father because my mother went to jail and I didn't want to go live in the city, because I didn't like it there. So the only alternative I had was to go live with my father, so I went to live with my father and it turned out okay, turned out perfect. I got allowances and stuff. It turned out perfect. A regular family. It was perfect. We had a pool, we had a two-car garage. It was like paradise. I didn't have to worry about where I was going to sleep the next time. I had clothes on my back. I had food in my mouth. My father really loved us. He took care of us, and so did my stepmother. Like I was her own son. . . .

My mother went to jail because she was sleeping and there were people coming in and out selling drugs out of the house. She didn't know. She was sleeping and then the cops raided the house. So that's why she didn't get that much time. She only got six months for being there. But my uncle got two and a half years. He went to the state prison. After six months they let my mother out. Then my mother got her old boyfriend to come stay with us. I can't stand that guy, Adam. He makes me sick. I can't stand him. If he comes here, I'll go and live with my father again. She got out of jail probably two weeks ago. A long time ago Adam was living with us, like when I was ten or twelve. I was about fourteen when she was sleeping and they were doing drugs in the house. I'm fourteen now. It was this past year. My birthday's going to be October 15th.

I didn't know they were doing drugs, because I used to live in Fairhale. I didn't know until they called me and told me. When I heard I didn't even want to listen to it. I just went about my business and went outside. And my aunt told me, "the house got raided" and I was like "so what, I don't care" and I just stepped outside. When I was in Fairhale I saw my mother. I used to live on Main Street, that was I think a half a mile from where I moved. I used to live in this old house near the high school, Fairhale High, and my mother lived upstairs from us. My father and stepmother lived downstairs, she lived upstairs. So I used to see her everyday before I'd go to school, until she moved, until she lived with my father's best friend. When my father's best friend moved she had to move. And I guess she moved back with her mother, my grandmother, and that's when she started doing drugs. And then we moved from there and then we bought our own house down in West Fairhale.

While she lived with Adam we lived in Forester Avenue. I don't like him because he thinks he was such a hotshot, saying "Oh yeah, I got money, I got money" and I go "So what?" I couldn't stand him so much I threatened I was going to kill him when I get older. He was such a big shot, he was like "Oh yeah, I got money, I got all this money, oh yeah." He used to flash money around. So what? I was like "I wish he'd get shot." The only person I liked was his cousin Tiny. Oh, he was the best friend you could ever have, Tiny. He was cool. After I threatened Adam and stuff, he moved out, because I was in access with the gangs out there and I threatened I was going to kill him and so he moved out and his cousin moved in. And at first I didn't like his cousin, either, because I thought they was cousins so they probably had the same ways, but then I really got to know him. We like took him out to eat and stuff. I got to know him and he was cool. And he was going out with my aunt. Tiny was going out with my aunt, Bea. And it worked out cool.

So I threatened Adam that I was going to kill him . . . because he made me sick. He used to act like he was my father and so that's when I said I'm going to kill him. I mean he knew I had access with the gangs. Because there was one gang on Santini Street in West Chelsbury and I had access with them, because I used to be with the Junior Santini until I moved and I quit from them. And so, they knew I was still down and he saw me like hanging with them. He knew I had access with them and he knew if he messed with me all I got to do is make one phone call and he would die. So, I had access with them.

I'm glad I'm away from the gangs. Because if I was with them now, the things they were doing now, if I was with them! Like, three days ago, my friend Clark called me. He's the head of Junior Santini, and he told me that they was walking across the street and a guy pulled up to a red light and he had his radio blasting, and he almost hit this guy, Philip, who was in the gang, and Philip kicked his car. The guy got out and started talking nasty and they just all shot him up. The Junior Santinis, the gang had guns. They always have guns on them, everywhere you go, because you don't know who's who. For all they know Philip could be a traitor. Philip could be with the D.C. gang. If he was, they'd have to shoot him. They'd have to kill him for betraying. Either way, he's going to die, either the Santinis are going to kill him or the D.C. gang's going to kill him. He wasn't going to live. I mean, I don't like all that killing. As my father said if I was out there a while longer, if I was out there today, I would be dead. He said he's glad I changed my life. I believe him. I think that's very true, I wouldn't be here today. . . .

We were about to visit some of my friends, me and my cousin, so she told me and my uncle Ray to meet them on the corner at eight o'clock. So we get at the corner at eight and they were right there. So one drug dealer comes up and goes "Hey man, what are you doing, trying to clock my block?" He thinks we're selling drugs on his turf. And so, he goes "What if I shoot you?" and I go "You know Junior Santini?" and they go "Yeah" and I'm like, "What if I get them to shoot you?" and he goes "Oh, oh, you down with them?" I'm like, "Yeah." He's like, "Oh, I'm sorry. I'm sorry" and I was like "Yeah, you better be." So everybody knows about them. Junior Santini takes over West Chelsbury. There's the Junior Santini and there's the Big Santini. The Big Santini, they all are in jail. My cousins, Paul and Mel, they were the head of Big Santini and they were at this party and a guy tried to shoot Paul. Mel shot the guy up thirty-two times in his head. So, then this other guy tried to jump in, too, so Paul shot him twelve times in the side. Now they're in prison. They're both in prison doing fifteen to thirty years. Those were cousins on my father's side, so he's glad to get us out of there.

I haven't been in one fight in four years out in Fairhale. In my old school I was in fights every day. Every day I used to have a fight. I used to bring all the problems I brought from home to school. I don't know, some kid would make a joke I didn't like and I would beat him up. But all the kids was taller than me. I was the shortest. Now look how tall I am. When I got to Fairhale it was different because everybody knew what I was feeling out there. They knew what was going on. My father knew what was going on. Because my father's niece, Reena, she died. Her husband killed her, stuck her in the trunk. So after the funeral my uncle said he was going to shoot him, kill him after the funeral was over. Luckily, my grandmother on my father's side, talked him out of it and then like three days later, after she talked him out, she died. Of a heart failure. . . .

If I had to tell something to kids who have to come to a shelter I would
just tell them to look on the brighter side. But, I don't know what the
bright side is. I hope my mother's not going to have to be here for long.
She will be until she gets an apartment I guess. I don't know how long
that will be. Some of these kids been here for a year. It won't be that
long for us because when school starts back, I'm going to go back with
my father until my mother gets an apartment, if she doesn't have an
apartment by then. She doesn't know that now, but she will find out when
I'm gone. I'm going to tell her at dinner. She can't say nothing, because
all I gotta do is put up that line, because I don't wanna go to school out
in here. The line I'm putting up is that I'm not staying here. Then after
I say that I'll leave. I go down the street and call my father and he'll go
"I'll be right there in ten minutes." My father only let us come because
my mother wanted to see us, because we haven't saw my mother in a
year. So he thought it best for we to come stay with her for a little while.
I think he was right but, I'm not sure.

COMMENTARY

Substance abuse and violence are a part of the stories of a number of
children who become homeless. Some, like Kendra and Dana, endure
substance abuse or violence in their immediate families. For others, the
experience is somewhat more indirect, occurring in the hallways, streets,
or neighborhood where they had been living. When the abuse or violence
is part of the fabric of the family, it is often a major contributor to eventual
homelessness. For Kendra, homelessness came at the end of many years
of unstable living situations, resulting from the alcohol addiction of both
parents. Dana also lived in multiple situations consequent to his mother's
drug addiction. Her addiction led to jail for her and now a shelter for
her and her children. Both Kendra and Dana, in different ways, have
experienced the violence that is not caused by, but is often associated
with, substance abuse. Many homeless children have experienced violence, either in their neighborhood or within their families. Similarly,
many have witnessed substance abuse, either in their immediate environment or in their household.

Violence in Neighborhoods

Prior to coming to the shelter, many children have lived in neighborhoods where violence has become commonplace. These children have
witnessed violence in its various forms. Often, this violence has contrib-

uted to their homelessness, either directly or indirectly. Ten-year-old Raymond, who moved to the United States from Haiti, described the situation in his native country: "Almost every night the guns have been firing. I guess we left Haiti because we wanted to have a good time." Troy described the violence in his previous inner-city neighborhood:

My old street wasn't that peaceful. Cops used to tell you to get in your house and stuff and you're just standing out there relaxing, getting some air or something. They would tell you to get in your house. Then I really didn't have nothing to do. People shooting off guns and stuff. I'm glad I'm not there at my old street.

Many children have lived in poor urban neighborhoods where violence in the streets has almost become commonplace. Often the children recount these stories with a sense that violence is frightening, but not unusual. Five-year-old Javier narrated the following account of a walk home from school in his old neighborhood: "One day, me and my mother, she picked me up from school and we were walking and saw a cop. He shot a bad man in the leg. I was scared. I don't know what the man was doing. We just saw half of it because we ran."

For twelve-year-old Bethany, the shooting in her neighborhood had become so routine that she and her siblings incorporated it into their play, much to their mother's dismay.

I might pretend I got shot. I was playing and one day when my mother was helping my sister get dressed, and I think it was my brother and me and my sister, we heard gun shots and we made pretend we were dead and we were laying on the floor and my mom goes "Stop it! Stop it!" because we were only playing. I don't get scared or worry about getting hit, because I'm never next to the window.

With a certain matter-of-factness, Bethany describes what for her is a simple solution to a life-threatening problem.

Family Violence

For many children, the physical violence strikes closer to home. Some children recount in detail the physical violence that occurred in their families, often remembering a single incident as the one that led to the breakup of the family and their becoming homeless. Even five-year-old

Maysa had a vague sense that their journey to the shelter began with a fight. "My daddy was fussing and my mommy was crying. My mommy packed up the clothes. And she went away." Many of these children have watched in horror as their fathers or their mothers' boyfriends had "hitting fights with my mother." Many of these children have mothers who were battered by abusive boyfriends or spouses and fled to a shelter in an attempt to save themselves and their children. Eight-year-old Kevin claimed that he did not know where the shelter was located. "My mother does not want me to know the street or the phone number. She said she wouldn't tell me because my father could get her and hurt her bad." While this child had every opportunity to determine at least the street name simply by reading the street sign, it is significant that he chose not to do so. He felt the need to protect his mother and himself and believed his lack of knowledge of the address would help them to remain safe.

Children experience extreme vulnerability during these incidents. They remember how frightened they were for their own safety. Ellie, who is eight, tearfully described her father attacking her mother with a "big shiny knife" during the previous year.

> It was awful. He got on top of her on the floor and he had this knife and he kept saying he was going to kill her. He was drunk like he always gets. My sisters and me, we did 911. I was scared. I was crying. My sisters were crying too. The police took him to jail. He was mad at us, but he got out the next day. But he was still mad at us.

Some of these children have not only witnessed violence but have been the victims of violence. A number have been physically or sexually abused. While most young children find this a very difficult area to speak about, some of the older children, particularly adolescents, seem to find some relief in the telling. Elizabeth recounted her tale of abuse, which began when she came home late one day:

> I went home and my father told us we had to go up to our room and we got in the door and my father hit us because he was mad. We were told to be home before it got dark and so we told my father why and then he sent us up to our room, me and my sister. . . . And then, the next day, we went to the doctor's. My sister went to the nurse's office at the school and told, complaining that her back hurt where my father had hit her. And her nurse checked it out and there was a big welt mark. So they came and they called me down at my

school and they checked my leg but it was fine. I just had a little, kind of bruise or a scratch or something, I forgot. And then a child abuse person came to our house the next day and talked to us about how we felt and if it hurt and everything, alone in the dining room. . . . And my father just got a warning about hitting us or something. . . . That's one thing that I always couldn't forget about what happened with me and my dad. He scared me that day.

Barbara, pregnant at seventeen, had been a runaway since eleven years of age. She reports that she ran away at such a young age because of "drugs, guns, alcohol, and abuse." Both parents were drug-involved. She described how her father, a Vietnam veteran, would mix alcohol with his psychotropic medication.

He spazzed out and went crazy. It was scary. He'd beat up on me and my mother and hold guns to us. And one time he held a gun to my head and told my mother that if she came any closer he was going to kill me. I was seven. I was scared. I thought he'd really do it. My mother left the house. He put away the guns after that and apologized. And then a couple hours later he overdosed with whiskey and these pills he was on. The ambulance and the police came and he beat up a couple of the police officers and they took him out in restraints. And that's when all this stuff started happening.

For Barbara "this stuff" meant years of domestic violence between her parents, and years of physical and sexual abuse by her parents.

Children respond to this repeated exposure to violence in a number of ways. In their stories, these children present a heightened sense of vulnerability and subsequent hypervigilance. Children repeatedly mention "people who might get me" or "people that hit kids." Although these children often do not share stories of their actual experiences with violence, themes of a vague sense of personal danger pervade their stories. For example, seven-year-old Raphael stated that he liked the shelter because "nobody hits me. There's bad people that hit kids and take kids too. They're not at the shelter. They're out there, everywhere." Troy was similarly a fearful little boy. Thankful for a variety of the shelter's safety features, Troy's sense of the world as a dangerous place was evident in his statement: "A curfew here is good, because kids aren't supposed to be out past eleven o'clock or they could get hurt. Because somebody could ride by and shoot them, like somebody speeding or something and they might get hit or something."

Often, these children express a sense that they are powerless to protect themselves and must rely on external defenses. For Troy, this means guards at the shelter doors. For Vicky security is brought by fences around the shelter, which keep people out. For many children the ultimate protection comes from their mothers. It is these children who express relief that the shelter provides what they see as an opportunity for their mother to stay home and not work. They are among the significant number of children, usually under ten years of age, who feel that their mothers could not work because if they did, the children would become certain victims of the people and the world "out there."

There are other children for whom the constant assault on their sense of security leads to intense anger and bitterness. Their faith and trust in those around them has been shattered. Since they cannot rely on anyone to protect them, they protect themselves. These sentiments are revealed between the lines of the children's stories. Themes of anger pervade some children's entire stories. These are children on the defensive.

Substance Abuse in Families

Substance abuse has managed to insinuate its way into the life of some homeless families. Children are quite aware of any substance abuse that has occurred among family members and friends. They express sadness and sometimes anger about the situation, and sheer helplessness to do anything about it. Some have lived with one or both parents who are alcoholics, and describe the frustration and pain of constantly trying to make their parents stop. Many of these children have grown tired and simply have given up.

Some children are even aware of the way in which they have reacted to the pain of an addicted parent. A few adolescents, such as Barbara, describe how they themselves became substance abusers as a consequence of what they had experienced as younger children. Ian, whose story contains references to gang violence, domestic abuse, and familial drug use, traced his history of violent behavior to these incidents:

I used to take fits because my uncle used to do cocaine in front of me in the house I used to live in when I was young. And like they'd always have cocaine parties and stuff. My mother was stupid enough to let them. I don't know why. That's what happened. They acted crazy then. And I used to see them. Not me, they didn't do nothing

to me, but I used to see them get in fights all the time and stuff.
Like rumbles. They'd get in fights with other people on the streets
and stuff. And I'd sit there and watch them. And I'd help. I threw
rocks at them.

Many children in this situation are acutely aware of what is happening
but are unable to talk about it, particularly with a parent who might be
an abuser. As a sixth grader, Haydn was exposed to his mother's drug
use. He stated:

I found out because I'd seen—I'd seen and my dad told me and, I'd
seen them doing all kinds of things. I don't want to say what I've
seen. I don't want to say what I've seen at all. But I've seen and I
know what I've seen. Because I've seen many things in school about
it, many things and everything from kids. My friends knowing more
than I know, because they lived in bad neighborhoods and they knew.
I learned from them. I was going in sixth grade then. My friends
were pretty smart. I knew bad stuff was going on. I knew. I knew
everything that was going on. I'd just never say anything. I'd just
watch. I didn't say anything to my mom. I'd just watch and I'd say
to myself that I would never let that happen to me.

Parental substance abuse may also be an ongoing concern. Although most
children steadfastly maintain that their parents have their addictions or
abuse problems under control, there are parents whose problems persist
into the shelter situation. Understandably, these parents have a substan-
tially decreased ability to meet their children's needs. Insofar as substance
abuse contributes to homelessness, families struggling with these issues
remain vulnerable to further instability in living situations until these
problems are addressed.

Substance Abuse in Neighborhoods

Drugs are a common problem in urban neighborhoods, and young
children are constantly exposed to them. Jose stated that his family left
their previous neighborhood due to drugs:

I know there were drugs just seeing the people. Like if you go down
the corner there's a lot of people using drugs. And like a lot of
people using alcohol. I know by the window, you see by the window.
I see people, fooling around and giving some drugs to the other

people. No needles. Only like pot, cocaine, all that stuff, but no
needles.

Jose went on to do what many school-age children living in drug-ridden
neighborhoods do, that is, talk to themselves about the evils of drug use.
"I couldn't get drugs because my mother wouldn't let me. I wouldn't. It
would just destroy my life. You can get it by just talking to another guy,
the guy could just go and get it." Isabella talked about her old neighborhoods and how "they were bad because of all the drug stuff and
everything. It wasn't good living in places like that."

These children sense their vulnerability and the pressure that living in
such a neighborhood presents. For this reason, many are glad for the
relative safety of the shelter and the protection they feel it affords—even
though, the shelter is often located in a similarly violent and drug-ridden
area of the city.

Responding to Violence and Substance Abuse

Because of the pain the incidents of family violence and abuse cause
children, many desperately seek to make meaning out of their experience.
Some are open and direct about their anger and feel that they have been
betrayed. Others prefer to say nothing, to ignore quietly whatever they
can. Dana chose to "shut down," or close himself off from the events
unfolding around him. When told that his mother was arrested for doing
drugs, he said "I didn't even want to listen to it. I just went about my
business and went outside. And my aunt told me, 'The house got raided'
and I was like 'So what, I don't care' and I just stepped outside."

Many children assert that they would never allow this to be done to
their children, that they will be their own children's protectors. This is
the case for Barbara, who expresses a feeling that her current pregnancy
is an attempt to compensate for love she never received as a child. "It's
mine and nobody could take it away from me. I can give it the love that
I missed."

Others, particularly children who are approaching adolescence, and
are reflecting on the years of hurt, try to find explanations for their
parent's behavior. Haydn explained that his mother's substance abuse
occurred "because of the type of people that she hanged around and the
type of environment that we were in and the type of friends, friends she
chose to have at that time. She made some wrong decisions."

Barbara reflected back on an incident in which her father tried to
strangle her mother. "At the time," she recalled "I was just scared. I

mean, in a way, I thought my mother maybe deserved it. . . . Because I thought maybe when you did something wrong and you had to pay for it." She tried to make sense of the physical violence between her parents, but became confused. "I just get all mixed up when I start thinking about it. I don't know. It's just sometimes I wonder if it was ever meant, if they did it on purpose, or if they're both just really sick." As for her own abuse, she expressed a feeling that "sometimes I don't even think that I really mattered to them." Nevertheless, Barbara concluded that her mother must have cared somehow. "I mean, I know in her own way she loves us. Even if she didn't, why would she have kept us, hide things from the child abuse social workers. If she didn't love us, she probably would have let the social workers take us."

Some children look back and try to come up with acceptable explanations for the substance abuse or violence. And some are hopeful that things can still change. Haydn notes that his family's move out of the city was his mother's attempt to remove herself from bad influences. Haydn expressed faith in his mother's ability to change. "She's going to make it. I know she's going to make it, because she's made it before."

Domestic violence and substance abuse can be precipitants to homelessness. In cases where domestic abuse was contained within the parental unit, the ramifications are still great for children. A woman who is abused may become depressed, apathetic, emotionally distant, or display passive and helpless behaviors. Children who are too young to understand the strength it took for their mother to survive in a violent situation, or the difficulties surrounding an escape, may come to see their mother as ineffective. Likewise, a drug-involved parent is likely to be less accessible to the children, due to the nature of the addiction. Seeing parents under these conditions may further heighten children's sense of vulnerability. It may also contribute to bitterness about not having their needs met, or increase the children's drive to protect their mothers.

There are a number of families for whom domestic violence or substance abuse had never previously been an issue. Yet the strains associated with and leading up to homelessness may have served as precipitating causes. Family tensions may have led to an eruption of violence. Parents may take out their own anger, frustration, and loss on their child. Once-manageable stressors inherent in raising children may become too difficult to manage. This is especially likely in a situation where children's needs for nurturance and protection are increasing as parental resources are decreasing. Substance abuse may be a last attempt to cope in what seems to be a no-win situation.

Children in these families are left to assimilate the changes in their families, such as violence, separations, home loss, or substance abuse. In the words of one six-year-old girl,

I don't know what happened. It seems like ever since I turned five my whole family isn't a family anymore. My grandmother's in Texas. My dad is in jail and he's not allowed to visit us anymore. And my mom never reads to me like she used to. Only when the worker comes over, then she reads to me. (Susan)

Chapter Eight

"Waiting for Grammy to Call": Family Relationships

JAVIER

Javier, age seven, his five-year-old sister, and their parents moved to their current location from a large midwestern city. The father is currently planning to go into the service in the hopes of obtaining training for a job. The mother and two children have been in the shelter for a week. The shelter only accepts women and children. They came to the area in an attempt to escape the violence and problems of the city and stayed with the father's sister prior to coming to the shelter. The sister was just starting out in the area herself, and it became too difficult for them to share a place. They all subsequently moved to a motel, where the aunt and father remain.

I came here from Chicago and I've been here six days. See these teeth missing? Four gone. They came when I was five, these teeth. Up top, those went out when I was six. When it's May 4, I'll be seven. That already happened. I'm seven now.

We left Chicago because it was all messy and everything. It was dirty. There was a lot of bad people all around. Cops everywhere. The bad people were robbing stores and everything. . . . Chicago was dirty. There was a lot of garbage and everything in the street. My house was a little bit clean. Not dirty inside, but dirty outside. Inside nothing was broken. The floors were okay. My mom kept it clean. We came to here because it's clean. And there's no robbers.

We came in a truck. We got it from the U-Haul place. My father and me in the passenger seat, and my mother and my aunt, and my sister was in the car. It was a long time driving. I was not that much scared. I was a little scared of all the bad people and everything. Bad people might be coming in here. I didn't know what it would be like. When we came we lived in Jameston with my mother, my father, and my aunt and Doreen. . . . We moved from Jameston because the lady who selled us the house, she wanted to sell it again. We had to get out of there. We came here because there was nowhere else to go. I don't know about why. My father's not here. He lives with my aunt and they're living in a motel, because there's not much space nowhere else. I don't know why he's not with us. I'd like it better if he was here. He comes a little bit every day. I miss him. I don't know how long we'll be living here. My mommy will get another place to live. We need to wait because she doesn't have a check of her money. When she gets it we'll be able to go to another house.

I speak Spanish. I can say everything in Spanish. In school I learn in English. I'm American. My mommy's American too. We speak Spanish and English. I watch TV. I don't have no favorite program. Only one. I forgot that name. I wish that I could get a new bike. And a new house. In my new house I'd have a separate room for my sister and me. And my father and my mother would live in a separate room too. And my aunt. It would have a kitchen and a bathroom and that's it. It would be in the country, not the city. I like the beach here and the swimming.

STEPHANIE

Stephanie is a ten-year-old girl who is currently living with her father and stepmother. Her mother lives in Utah and her stepsister, the child of her mother, lives in Georgia. She has a younger brother, Willy, who is nine years old and the son of her stepmother. Her family came to the area to visit Stephanie's paternal grandfather. They spent a few days in the home of her father's first wife and then moved into a hotel. They have been in the shelter for two weeks. This family's history has been characterized by multiple moves all over the country. They have lived in shelters many times.

I'm ten years old. My brother's nine. We've been at Harbor House not very long because we was at North Street Motel before. We came from Texas back here. Besides living in this state twice, we've lived in Texas and California and Nevada and Georgia. My favorite place for living is Georgia. My sister lives there and she has a baby and she wants to see me and my other mother wants to see me. My other mother lives in Utah. She's my real mom. This mom is my stepmother. And this dad is my real dad. I lived with my real mom not very long. I went to my dad because he just wanted me. He just didn't want her to have me. I don't know why, because I was little. I didn't care because we went to his dad and his mother up here and I liked it because they had a pool at the motel and we swammed in it. My sister in Georgia is my real mom's daughter. I think she's in her twenties. She's married and she has a baby. I haven't seen her since we lived in Georgia. I was eight then. I could visit her then. She came down and picked me up. And we went back to her and she lives in Atlanta. My real dad is her step-dad. It's hard to keep it straight. . . .

My brother doesn't like moving either. Because in Texas he liked it down there and when he moved up here he was mad because we moved. And he liked it in California because his grandmother was there and he lived with her. We had to leave when it snowed. My parents said so. We moved because we were going to Texas. We have to move so much because some spots we don't like and some spots we like. My mother and father decide to move and then we tell them what we want. . . . I'd live in Georgia if I could.

I met some kids. Up here in North Seton school the first day I made friends and down there they were like not friendly and stuff. When we have to leave and we have friends, we missed them a lot. I write them a little. They don't write me. It's hard living in a lot of places. In Nevada we didn't go to school. My dad was gone and my mother was living with her daughter in Nevada. Dad was in the Army. And we missed him a lot. He was in the Army ten years. Sometimes it's a little hard having two moms. Because when we moved here from Georgia and I was up here and she called us and she wanted me. She wanted to see me but I couldn't go because there wasn't no way I could have gone down there. I haven't seen my real mom since I was a little kid. And then when she lived in Georgia I seen her when I was eight and seven. I don't have any pictures of her. I write. Not very much. She writes me once in a while. I tell my stepmom that it makes me sad. I only tell her a little. She says "Well you probably will see her but not right now." When I get big, I'm going to go to Georgia to see my sister and then get a job. . . .

Sometimes I get mad that we have to move so much. I tell my dad or my mom. Sometimes I tell them. They say "We won't move but we have to move sometimes." Then we move a lot of times. Because sometimes my stepmother wants to go see her mother and my dad wants to like come up here and see Gramps and in Georgia he was living there and I was born there. And we went down there for some reason. There's always a reason, like to go see somebody. When I get big I think I'm going to live in one place. I've been in like five schools in three grades. That's been pretty a lot.

I wish that we can go down to Georgia to see my sister and then go to see my real mother.

COMMENTARY

The shelter in which Javier lives admits only mothers and children. For Javier, such a rule is hard to comprehend, and he expresses sadness and confusion over the fact that his father is not living with him. He offers a guess that his father's absence is related to a lack of space, and subsequently expresses a wish that his family will soon have a home where his parents can have a room of their own. Javier's need to be close to his father is evident in his recounting of the family's move. For example, he is careful to state that he was seated with his father in the passenger seat during their travels.

Unlike Javier, whose separation from his father is related to the circumstance of being homeless, Stephanie is struggling with a more permanent separation and loss. Many homeless children live with only one parent, usually the mother. Stephanie's case, in which she lives with her natural father and her stepmother, is less typical, but the dynamics are similar. Her desire to be in contact with her mother is frustrated by the sense of distance, both physical and emotional, that she feels is between them. She wants to visit, but rarely writes her.

Like all families, the homeless family reflects the culture in which it is embedded. The traditional American family is changing:

> The description in our first grade primers of father at work and mother at home caring for their children applied to only 22 percent of American families in 1981. A spiraling divorce rate, increasing poverty, pregnancies to unmarried teenagers, and changing work patterns are among the factors that contribute to a dramatically different portrait of the American family today. (Dubowitz, Newberger, Melnicoe, and Newberger, 1988)

Reflecting this larger picture, the structure of homeless families is often complex. Most often, these families are headed by the mother. The father of the children may be in touch or living close by; he may be at a significant distance, or even be unknown to the child. In many families, the children are stepsiblings. In a few cases, the parent with whom the child lives may not be the biological parent. Many of the single mothers have partners, who have varying levels of involvement in the life of the family and the children.

A number of children have grandparents, aunts, uncles, cousins, or other relatives to whom they are attached to varying degrees. Like all families, homeless families vary in terms of their closeness to one another. Physical proximity to the extended family differs between families. In some cases, a majority of extended family members live in the same neighborhood, town, or city. Other homeless families are more distant from extended family members, living in a different city, state, or even country. Homeless families also differ from one another in terms of their psychological ties to extended family members; some are extensively bonded to individuals in their extended family, while others have no close ties to other relatives. As one would expect, the physical distance does not seem to be a critical factor in how close family members are.

Family relationships are often profoundly affected when families become homeless and move to a shelter. These changes in family relationships are the result of changes in either the structure or function of the family.

Changes in Family Structure Contributing to Homelessness

Changes in family structure often occur when a family becomes homeless and finds itself in a shelter or motel. Becoming homeless and moving into a shelter means, for children, not just a change in living place and a loss of friends and possessions, but also changes in the composition of the immediate family. These changes may be temporary or permanent.

Some of these changes may have actually caused the family to end up in a shelter. Relationships between a mother and her boyfriend or spouse may suddenly end. Separations or divorces can greatly deplete or exhaust a family's financial resources. The shelter is often their only recourse. Other times, choices are made by mothers to move in order to escape an abusive husband or boyfriend. Still other mothers may move to pursue a relationship, that is, be closer to an ex-husband or boyfriend, having received a signal of some kind that things could possibly work out. These moves result in their being without housing and without money when they arrive at their destination.

The alterations in family structure that these changes involve are often very difficult for the children to manage. Charlie's mother, after splitting up with her current boyfriend, moved thousands of miles to be near her ex-husband, who is Charlie's father. Her ex-husband had indicated to the mother that things between them could get better. The hoped-for mending of the relationship did not materalize. Charlie's hopes that the pain of leaving his mother's boyfriend, to whom he was very attached, would be ameliorated by renewed contact with his biological father were dashed. Charlie and his mother were living in a welfare motel for months waiting for housing, with no money to "go back home." Charlie spent a significant amount of his time poring over the photo album they had brought with them of the mother's ex-boyfriend, whom he considered his dad. "There's me with dad. There's me and dad with Aunt Joanie. There's me with dad and my grandma. There's me diving with my dad." The change in family structure was difficult for this young child. Being homeless and thousands of miles away served to intensify his pain.

T. J., the oldest of six children, is in a shelter because his mother just separated from her second husband, T. J.'s stepdad. Dana and his brother Haydn left a contented life with their father and stepmother to join their natural mother, who had recently been released from prison. It was hoped that their presence would help their mother get a housing certificate more quickly in order to restart her life.

Jose's mother separated from his dad many years ago, and recently separated from her boyfriend of several years, whom Jose considered "my real dad sort of." After the second separation, the mother was trying to start life again in another city, and went into a shelter with her four children because she could not afford housing. Jose said:

My dad is in Puerto Rico. I usually don't see him. When I was in Puerto Rico for this past year I saw him. He lives near my grandma. I was glad to see him. He's the dad for me and my brother. My little sister and brother, their dad is the one that we just moved from. I like him. I like him as a father. I miss him a lot. He didn't go to Puerto Rico with us because his mother was dying. She needed an operation and he couldn't go with us. I don't know if he's going to come live with us in this new place. I don't think so. He lives with his mother now. We didn't see him or call him since we came back from Puerto Rico. I still miss him. He was like a dad. My dad in Puerto Rico lives with another woman. He has kids. Two are my half brother and sister. I met them, they're okay.

Changing relationships can leave children very confused, particularly young children, who are not yet able to understand what has happened. In describing her father and mother's separation, Valerie, who is five, tried to make sense out of the changes in the relationship. "My mother doesn't like my dad anymore. She gets mad at him. My grandma is mad at him. My brother is at my grandpa's. My dad is coming back. He's going away." In trying to understand what is happening to these relationships, children's descriptions reflect the confusion they experience. Four-year-old Daniel, whose mother recently separated from his father, described the situation as follows:

We had to move because my father and mother said so. The house was no good because I didn't like it and mommy and dad didn't like it either. Because it was no good, because that's why when they get mad they didn't like it. They didn't like it this way and that way. . . . We came here because I lived with my dad and my mother, and, not with my father, but my father lived where the dump trucks are. He isn't living here. He already has a house. I don't live in his house.

Changes in Family Structure Resulting from Homelessness

In contrast to family changes that precipitate a family's coming to the shelter, some of these changes in family structure are the consequence of having come into the shelter. Finding a place to live together is often difficult, and many families must separate. Various shelters prohibit men, infants, or teenagers. Other family members do not come to the shelter because they do not want to come, as is often the case with older children. Those family members who do not come to the shelter may be staying with a relative, former spouse, or friend, or they may be in foster care. Most often, the person not present is the father of the children. In other cases, living in the shelter has resulted in separation from siblings, particularly older siblings on whom the child relied. Jose feels strongly the absence of his brother, who remained in Puerto Rico with his grandmother in order to finish the school year. Jose's life now revolves around his return. "Now I'm just waiting for him. I miss him. We talk by the phone. This month he gets out of school. He'll be coming then. He wants to come. He's good." Seven-year-old Gertie talked about her older sister, who is fifteen and is living in different place because "she does not want to live in the shelter."

Coming to the shelter often results in increased separation from relatives who were not living with the family, but were close by when the family was living in another section of the city or another state. This separation is part of the pain children try to deal with in the shelter. Many families in the shelter are at a greater physical distance from ex-spouses or ex-partners than they were in their previous home. Consequently, the children have less contact with these ex-partners who are their parents or step-parents. Coming to the shelter has made many children more physically distant from their dad. Those who are living with their biological father may become more distant from their mom.

Coming to the shelter also may mean that children become separated from extended families. Separation from grandmothers seems to be a particularly painful issue for children in shelters. Jose stated: "My grandmother in Puerto Rico, she calls me sometimes. One day a week. She misses me and I miss her. I don't know what she thinks about us being in the shelter." Mrs. Rodriguez, the mother of five children under eight, had been given a one-way bus ticket by welfare authorities in her state and moved her family over a thousand miles to follow a boyfriend. With no resources, she and her family lived in a shelter waiting to get into subsidized housing. The dominant theme in her children's conversations, both individually and together, revolved around how much they missed their grandmother, who had lived near them in their old house. In another family of five, housed in a small room in a welfare motel, the major event of the week was "waiting for Grammy to call." Even the twenty-month-old got her turn at the phone. It is evident that, for many of these children, grandmothers have played a particularly nurturing role in their lives, and the separation was very difficult.

Even for families whose relatives do not live far from the shelter, the physical separation can be significant. The structure of the shelter, the lack of space, and the crowded conditions make having visitors particularly difficult. For these reasons, many shelters discourage visitors, limiting access of relatives. In other situations, the shelter address may be kept secret from extended family members. For example, a mother may not want an ex-partner to locate her. In some cases, extended family members do not like the concept of a shelter and refuse to visit there. Ian remembered vividly that "my grandmother wouldn't come to the shelter for my birthday."

Contact with relatives can also be limited by other circumstances. Very few families in the shelter have transportation. Consequently, visiting one's family can be very difficult. Even phone contact with extended family members can be difficult in the shelter. The single phone for the shelter residents is usually overbusy, or the shelter may have rules about calling out, particularly if there is a charge involved. Vicky described the situation in her shelter: "They've got phone limits. Ten minutes. Fifteen minutes for adults. Five minutes for kids." Other children note the difficulty finding change to put in the pay phone. Whatever the cause, these limitations of contact with extended family members to whom the child is attached add to the stress of homelessness.

Sometimes coming to the shelter may not result in a separation. Yet for children who have experienced significant separations in the past, the precarious nature of shelter living may evoke a flood of memories about earlier separations. Barbara, who lived in a family fraught with domestic violence and drug abuse, recalled her relationship with her grandmother, a source of comfort for her:

I was real close to her. She used to live with us. And my dad beat her up a couple of times. She'd tell us, well at night we'd sit up and talk, and she'd tell me that someday we're going to take ourselves, move to Las Vegas. And just about that time we got the money saved up to go, she passed away.

Changes in Family Functioning in the Shelter

Homeless children also experience changes in how the family functions. Changes occur in terms of the emotional closeness or distance between themselves and their parents, in terms of the roles that family members play, and in terms of the rules that govern the behavior of family members.

The change in closeness and distance is the result of the shifting emotional needs of individual members of the family. A shift in the psychological distance between parent and child may result from either the stresses of shelter living, particularly the small space allotted to each family, or the emergence of feelings in the child about becoming homeless, that is, anger and fear.

Physically, families in shelters and motels have much smaller personal living space than they did in their home. Families are typically assigned to a single bedroom in a shelter, with larger families sometimes able to have two bedrooms. This requires family members to spend a significant amount of time with each other in the same small space. It provides little opportunity for privacy or time to be alone, or even to do one's "own thing." This change in the dimensions of the physical living arrangements may alter the comfort level that the child had established within the old living arrangements.

For school-aged children and adolescents, the physical constraint can be emotionally taxing. Children complain about being unable to get away from other family members. Lisa, an adolescent, is living in a small motel room along with her younger brother, Sam, her mother, and her stepfather. She had previously lived in other shelters with her family, and struggled to understand the reasons for "all the fighting":

> Everybody in our family fights a lot around here and it upsets you. You know, they fight about little things. I mean, if somebody says something that nobody likes or if somebody's being too loud, somebody's being too quiet, you mess up something, you don't wash out the shower good enough. You know, little things. And it's like, the dishes, the sweeping, the housework. It's just, a lot of little things throw things off. Like, the fact that when the checks come in and everything, you know, everybody's happy then. If you're not extremely happy you have to be fighting or something. I mean, it just somehow works that way. It seems like those are the two extremes. That's the way people are. If you can't be happy, I mean you get really depressed. I do. I get really depressed because I think about Minnesota and I wish I was there. And then again I'm glad I'm here because of the friends I've met, the people I met, I don't know. This whole motel situation, it gets upsetting but I can deal with it because I've dealt with a lot worse. Like divorce, not seeing my father. But you get really touchy, but, I don't know, sometimes I fight back. If somebody says something to me I fight back, right back to them.

Lisa's brother, Sam, also understood the relationship between the crowded living situation and the fighting:

> The worst part about living in a place like this is if you want to go to sleep and people are awake and they just don't get along very well. It's too crowded. Everybody wants to be the boss. That's all. It makes for fights. We don't fight that much, but it's just nasty. When things get bad, I just go in the bathroom and calm down, you know. Because I get really mad. I have a bad temper. It just doesn't show. I do something else too. I try to make everybody happy by letting people do what they want when I know that I don't want to do it, but, I do it anyway.

Changes in the psychological distance between parent and child may be the result of not only the physical situation of the shelter, but also the emotions that becoming homeless and moving into a shelter bring to the surface, such as fear and anger. When they move into the shelter, children experience stress, which can often cause them to move either closer to or away from the parent. Landing in a shelter intensifies normal fears, especially in younger children. These children then make more demands on mothers to be nurturing, at a time when it is particularly difficult for the mothers. Similarly, finding themselves in a shelter can intensify the child's anger at the mother for, as many adolescents perceive it, not doing her job correctly and causing them to end up in a shelter. These feelings serve to distance them from their parents, who often report that the children have become more sullen and withdrawn or more difficult to talk to since they have come to the shelter.

Conversely, the circumstances of being homeless and in a shelter may create more closeness among family members, causing them to cling a little tighter to one another. The size and institutional quality of many shelters and motels may foster family cohesion as family members strive to maintain an identity. In a certain sense they seem to feel that it is their little family unit against the world. Children, particularly preschoolers and younger school-age children, tell of many close moments between themselves and their parents, particularly those moments when the child is able to share his or her sad feelings about being in the shelter.

In addition to changes in the psychological distance between family members, moving to a shelter often results in a change of roles in the family. Children are usually very aware that their mother is no longer doing "mother things." If the shelter provides the meals, the sheets for the bed, and the clothes (in the form of donations), and pays for the electricity and heat, children perceive that their mothers are not serving in their usual provider roles. Mother no longer shops for food or clothes, cooks, cleans, or pays the bills. This can be reassuring to children whose mothers had been unable to perform these functions very effectively, or conversely, quite threatening to those children who do not understand where that part of their mother has gone.

For many children, it is not only the mother's role that changes, but theirs also. Many children respond to becoming homeless and their inability to control their fate by assuming some of the parent's role. Their need to help their family control its fate intensifies their need to take charge. Children engage in role reversal in a variety of ways. Many children express concern about their parents' inability to manage the instrumental tasks of the family, for example, providing food or shelter, or managing money. Some children talk about how ineffective the parents are at tasks that revolve around pragmatic survival issues, and suggest steps for the parents to take. These children are worrying about the survival tasks in the family that adults usually worry about, such as finding a place to live. Nine-year-old Tucker's assumption of an adult role was revealed in his discussion of his mother's management of money:

> Well, usually she borrows money to buy some stuff. Then once she gets a check she has to repay everybody! And then she doesn't have any money left! I think she should don't borrow any more, but then we need some stuff because we got to buy a lot of food and we need to borrow some money! So we borrow some money and then my mother keeps on borrowing some, 'til it ends up to be a lot of money then they have to pay it back in a check. I would tell her she should or we're going to starve to death or something like that! Because if she needs some money for food, she's going to have to borrow it. She borrows it from my grandmother, my aunt and my uncle, the whole family. She doesn't have any money because my whole family says that she wastes her money on all sorts of things she don't need. Like she wastes it on a lot of candy for us. See, every time she gets a check she's like "Okay, I'm going to make my kids happy" but she makes us too happy. She buys us a lot of junk that we don't need like candy and stuff. Then it's all gone! I don't have to be happy that much! She makes us too happy.

Some children talk about assuming parental roles when they are adults themselves, and vow to do it differently. Marcus tells of his plans to "have a job and take care of my mother and sister and my brother. And my kids and my wife. We're going to have a home. We'll get it because I'm going to work real hard. And get a car." Marcus, like other children, is feeling a sense of responsibility that he cannot act upon.

Other children try to manage their parents' behavior, particularly regarding addictions. They may monitor a parent's behavior or serve as a source of moral support. A few children try to become money earners to do something about the family's plight. Sean describes saving every penny he found. Others plan jobs or tasks they could do for pay, such as babysitting.

In contrast, there are some children who are more resistant to assuming parental responsibilities. These kids resent the undue responsibility that is thrust upon them, such as caring for siblings. These feelings are intensified in cases where the child feels nobody did for them what they must do for others.

The functioning of the family also changes with respect to the rules that govern the family's behavior. The rules that now become central are the rules of the shelter, and often these are different from the parent's rules. Children perceive the difference and are frequently conflicted about how to make sense of them. For many children, the shelter staff seems to have assumed one of the central roles of the mother in determining the rules of behavior. Reprovals for violations are given by staff members. Many of the rules pertain to common activities in the shelter and are frequently more restrictive than the rules for the same activity at home. Rules about watching TV, for example, are often different from those at home. However, the rules about personal habits are often less restrictive in the shelter. In most cases, the shelter only makes bottom-line rules about personal behavior. However, children interpret these minimal rules as "the rule," and sometimes see them as less stringent than the requirements of home.

When the rules of the shelter override the rules of individual families, parental authority may be undermined, contributing further to the shifting of familial roles. In the shelter, mothering becomes a public matter. Parents must adapt their parenting style to the new rules and the constant scrutiny of others. Parents, whose emotional resources are exhausted, may simply throw up their hands. Ian recounted how he skips school:

> My mother's just been letting me stay home. She's not as strict. She doesn't want me to stay home. She just lets me if I bug her enough. Like if she kept saying "No" I would go. I wouldn't skip. She gives in too easy. That makes it hard for me. Any kid if they had a choice to stay home or go to school, they'd stay home.

For both parent and child, the shifting and changing of family relations is difficult to manage. These changes come at a time when the family is particularly vulnerable, and serve to heighten the pain and conflict surrounding the loss of a home. Homeless individuals need the social support of their family network more than ever, but homelessness often renders this support system less accessible.

Chapter Nine

"I Ain't Telling Them I'm in a Shelter": Friends

JOSE

Jose and his family are from Puerto Rico. His mother lived and worked in the United States for a number of years before her two sons joined her here. While they lived in this country, she had two children, a boy who is now twenty months and a girl now six months old. After the babies were born, she found it difficult to continue working and moved back to Puerto Rico. When they again returned to the United States, they went directly to the shelter and have been there for three months. Jose's fifteen-year-old brother stayed behind with his grandmother to finish the school year. They are now waiting for subsidized housing.

I turned twelve on April 8. I've been in the shelter two weeks, no two months. . . . Before this we lived in Puerto Rico just a year. Before that we lived in Tarton for seven years. Before that, Puerto Rico again. We were always in Puerto Rico before we came to Tarton. . . . Before that, in Puerto Rico, I lived with my grandma. My mom left for Tarton when I was like six or five. I was happy because I thought she was going to get a job. I wanted her to because in Puerto Rico there is not a job around. She wanted a job. I wasn't sad she was away because I was with my grandma. Then I had my brother who was older, but my little brother and sister were little though. He was like twelve. Now he's fifteen. He stayed with grandma too. . . .

When I was nine me and my brother came to Tarton. He was fourteen. We stayed there for three or four years. Then we went back to Puerto Rico, with my mother, my brother, my little sister and brother. They were born before we went back to Puerto Rico. We went back to see how things were over there. I was happy to go. I was a little sad to leave Tarton because of friends. And school was better in Tarton. I was slow in Puerto Rico school. I did better in Tarton. In Tarton there was a lot of kids, and teachers just seemed to be helping you with your work. I like to get help. In Puerto Rico I was slow because they just give you a job and they don't like help you or anything. And they didn't have computers, gym, all that stuff. At Tarton I had A's and B's. I had some special classes with special help for computers, making books, writing by myself. I liked that. When I went back to Puerto Rico I went to school and it was not good. Kids fighting all the time. Not me, but I didn't like it. I didn't make any friends. I didn't want to because then they get me in trouble, stuff like that. I went back there with my mother in our own place. She worked in Tarton until we left. . . .

I always been in Boys Club right after school. It's good. I like it. We gets to play baseball, basketball, all that stuff. It helps to not get on drugs just by staying in there. If you got in there you can't go out until you're finished a year. Then you don't get drugs. I don't go to the Boys Club here at the shelter. I don't know where it is. They said maybe I'll go when I move out. I'm moving out June 1st. Only my mother saw the apartment. She says it's got a big kitchen. She liked it. I got to the shelter on Monday and started school on Friday. Someone took me. It was a taxi. They just gave us a piece of paper at the shelter to show what we're going to take in school. That's where the taxi took me, to that school. And I started work. Going to a new school was sad and happy sometimes. It was sad learning all the new stuff and making friends. That felt not too happy. I made friends by talking to them. It's what you have to do. My teacher told everybody I was new, my name was Jose. My teacher helped me to make friends. I'm a big kid in my class. I know a friend, Toby. He's big too, big for eleven years old.

The shelter is good. They help you find houses and make your children be happy, take your children to school. We get happy here because men sometimes bring us to the library and let us take a book out. And they help us with homework. When I have homework I just go downstairs in the office, and they'll help you with it. A lady downstairs helps especially. I don't know the hard part about being here. I know it's good. There are no parts I don't like. Living here is not bad, but not good enough. It's not good enough because you got no friends in here. And they won't let you out. At five o'clock you have to be back in here. I'd like to be out 'til like six o'clock with my friend. I play with them after school. I go to his house. He knows I live here. He thinks nothing about it. He's Spanish like me. I speak Spanish and English. My friend knows things like that I'm new. He knows that I live here because I'm new around here. All the people live here to get apartments and a certificate. Don't ask me why they need to come here. . . .

My friend Toby, he thinks it's not pretty good that I'm living here. He says that if he moves out of his home, he'll maybe live here. But he won't move out of his place. He says he won't come here. I didn't tell him what it was like. He didn't ask me. I don't think he should come here! Not unless he doesn't have a place to live. It's sad when you don't have a place to live. It's bad. I don't know why. It's just bad. When I was coming to the shelter I thought "It's going to be good, better." I wasn't too much scared about coming. I was scared a little. I thought it would be like a new home, new friends, new school. . . . The first day here it was strange, because of people that I didn't know. The difference between a home and a shelter is you can't get the food you want at the shelter, you can't watch television 'til ten o'clock, you can't play, can't do nothing. Toby, my friend, can come over sometimes. He can come in, but only to the hall. He can't go upstairs. He can come over and see me on the weekends. He can call me here. I call him too. . . .

I play baseball and basketball. I like sports. I play on a big team for baseball. It's a Puerto Rican team. We all speak Spanish, plus the coach. I get there by walking. It's not too far. I don't have a bike, but maybe when I get an apartment I'll get one. I just want a skateboard, not really a bike. When I get big, I want to be a policeman. Right now I'd like to get a skateboard and have my brother come here and go to high school.

BETHANY

Bethany came to the shelter three days ago with her mother and two brothers. They were living out of state with the mother's boyfriend and his mother, and came here for a family celebration. In the interim, the boyfriend's mother communicated that she did not want them back. They then stayed with their maternal grandmother briefly, until she too asked them to leave. They have been in many shelters in the past.

I'm twelve years old. I'm in fifth grade, but I don't go to school right now because I just moved. Before we came here we were at my grandmother's house for a couple of days. Before that we were at Rhode Island. We were in Rhode Island for a long time. We left for the big family party. We left where we were living because we wanted to go to the celebration. We came up here. We came to the shelter because my grandmother didn't want us with her anymore. She didn't want us to wreck her house because she just cleaned it for the big celebration. . . .

In Rhode Island we were living with my father's mother. My father lived with us. He didn't come to the celebration. He stayed down there. He doesn't work there. He just lives down there. He lives with his mother and she didn't want us to come back. I don't know how long we lived there. Maybe it has been since I was in fifth grade. That was this year. Before Rhode Island we were living at my grandmother's house again, in this area. I don't know why we left there in the first place. I don't like moving like this. The worst part is that you make friends and then, the next day, you have to leave and leave your friends. That feels kind of sad because I miss my friend that's long, long, long gone. And her name is Sophia. She used to babysit me and stuff like that. I made kind of a lot of new friends. They're kind of close friends. I've been here just a few days, but I had friends from before. I made new friends in Rhode Island, not good friends, a little friends. It's hard to make new friends because there's hardly any kids outside. They were at school and I couldn't find new friends.

It's hard to get into school. I have a hard time getting into school because in Rhode Island you have to get a physical to get in, like going to the doctor to get a physical. It took a long time and I missed a lot of school. I think it was weeks. When we lived in Towbridge I always went to school. And then when I went to Rhode Island it got hard to get into school. The friends in Rhode Island didn't know that I was leaving, just going to the celebration. I didn't know we weren't going back until the day of the celebration. My mom told me. She said we're not going back because Francis, my stepfather, his mother doesn't want us back. I thought "It's okay." When my grandmother said we couldn't stay with her either my mom said "We're going to find a place." She said "We're going to the St. Anthony's Home until we find an apartment." I think she knew about this place since we started going to the day center. That was a long time ago. At the center we play and you eat and it's fun there. . . .

In school I do good. My best thing in school is spelling and the hardest is science and social studies. My teacher in Rhode Island doesn't know where I am, where I have gone. I don't know what she'd think. Kids will say "Where is Bethany?" Another kid will say "I don't know." So will my teacher. They'll all be wondering. I'm going to try to get into school here. But I don't like school. I don't like everything about it. Lunch or recess is okay. I like that. My teacher's okay. I liked it before sometimes. If you have to move like I do, it's worse. Moving everywhere. I've been almost all over the states. I've been in Rhode Island. Here we've just mostly been in this state, but in different places. It's hard to do. When you make friends and then the next day or a couple of weeks you have to move, it's bad. And what if it's a bad place or something. . . .

I'm the oldest. I don't like it. I have to do everything. I have to get my sister dressed. I have to do my sister's hair, get my brother's clothes and all that and not just since we've been here, but all the time. My mother gets supper in our house and does the wash. I have to sometimes sweep the floor, fold the sheets or anything, like fix the bed. I don't babysit. I would like to but I can't. I don't take care of my own brothers because my mother doesn't work. So she does it pretty much all the time. Sometimes we run out of money. Really nothing happens when we do. We have food. We don't get money, but in Rhode Island they have a church that gives food away, without paying it. So we do that. We came here instead of getting an apartment because we couldn't find an apartment.

COMMENTARY

Jose and Bethany are quick to relate that one of the most difficult aspects of moving frequently is the loss of friends. Bethany had to leave her old neighborhood and school without an opportunity to even say good-bye. Not only do these two children miss their former friends, they must struggle to make new friends. Shelter living and visitor rules can complicate this task even further.

Making and having friends is a significant part of the world of most children. Friends provide companionship, helping to fend off feelings of being alone and isolated. Friends also help children to understand and deal with the ups and downs of their existence, particularly those parts of their lives about which children find it difficult to talk to parents or other grown-ups. Although at different ages friends serve different roles for children, a good friend at any age is told and keeps many secrets, often about the most painful and difficult aspects of a child's life.

For children who become homeless, friends are often one of the first casualties of the situation. These children experience many impediments to maintaining lost friendships and forming new ones. Friends are left behind when a child moves from his neighborhood into a shelter or motel.

Furthermore, even under the best of circumstances, making new friends
is a challenge for most children. This task is particularly hard for
homeless children. Forming new friendships is difficult, whether inside
or outside the shelter. Even when friendships were previously formed
easily, when one is living in a shelter relating to peers in normal ways,
such as bringing a friend home, is often impossible. The embarrassment
of being homeless and living in a shelter keeps many homeless children
isolated.

Missing Old Friends

Friends are often left behind when a child moves from his neighborhood into a shelter or motel. Staying in touch with these old friends is
difficult or even impossible. Distance and lack of transportation, the
inaccessibility of phones or letter-writing materials, and embarrassment
about being in a shelter are some of the deterrents to maintenance of
friendships. Even if the shelter is a local one, not too distant from the
child's old home, younger children have no way to get back to old friends
on a regular basis. Children regularly report missing old friends. This
loss is large and painful for them.

Dana, who left his father's home to stay with his mother in the shelter,
detailed his experience:

It was hard for me to leave. It was. After I left, my friends started
coming over our house and asking where I was. My father said that
I moved. So I would try to call them and like they wouldn't answer.
So my father came over yesterday and I wanted to go over his house,
but he had to work early in the morning. I'm probably going because
he got a lot of people calling and asking about where I am and stuff,
because usually I'm up every day in the summertime. I'm out,
probably seven in the morning I'm over my friend's house and so
when they see me stop coming around one week, they was wondering where I am.

Doreen, who is five, described leaving her friends at school; during
the conversation, she switched to her feelings about leaving her mother
to go to school. The similarity of the feelings, the sadness at separation,
was obvious in her conversation.

When I left New York, I missed my other friends. I went to Head
Start and I want to live in Head Start. I was crying because I wanted

to stay there. I wanted to stay with my mother. I wanted to stay with my mother. I didn't want to stay at Head Start. Then I liked Head Start. When Mommy said "We're going to leave New York. We're going to go away," I said bye to all my friends. I said bye to everybody. They said bye to me. I can't see them. I told Mommy I was sad. I made new friends now. I have three friends here. Meri that's one and I don't remember who's two.

Nine-year-old Dominic lived in a motel with his mother, who had just finished an alcohol treatment program. The motel was about twenty-five miles from his old home. "It was better where I lived in Claremont because I knew more people. I was living there for a long time. I knew a lot of friends. Since I came here, I saw them once. I went back. My uncle took me. That was good. I miss them bad."

Embarrassment

Many children, not just those who are homeless, move and have to leave their friends. It is a consequence of living in a mobile society. Usually, kids who move are able at least to stay in touch with old friends who are far away. If the move is not too distant, visiting is an option. But children who become homeless often let old friendships slip rather than suffer the embarrassment of having to tell friends that their new address is a shelter for the homeless. After explaining how she wrote a letter to her old friend in Florida, Tara stated:

She didn't write to me. No, because she doesn't know my address. I never told her I was living in a shelter, because she'd open her big mouth. She'd tell everybody in the whole world I bet! And they would say a lot of bad stuff. Like "Oh, she lives in a shelter. You shouldn't be her friend!"

Isabella, who remained in her former school after moving to the shelter, described an elaborate scheme in which she led the children at school to believe that she still lived in her old apartment. She simply told them that she couldn't have company over to her house right now, "but maybe next week." She reported that the curtains and shades were still in the windows in the old place so that "the kids couldn't tell from the outside that no one lived there now." Her brother, who was older, used the same strategy. "If they knew I lived in a shelter they'd start teasing me like 'Ha ha ha ha. I have a home and you don't.' They still think I live in my

regular house. I just never invite them to my house. I used to before I
came to the shelter." Dana, too, strove to hide the nature of his move
from his friends.

> Well, I was so shocked that I was going to be living in a shelter, I
> just told him I'm going to the youth detention center. They go "Okay.
> See you when you get back." That's what I told them. I didn't want
> to tell my friends that I was going to a shelter or tell my girlfriend
> that I was going to a shelter. I'd feel like an idiot. My friends are
> thinking "Homeless." So I just tell them I was going to youth
> detention and they said "See you when you get back." Being
> homeless, that's not cool. People knowing you're homeless, your
> friends, that's not cool. I was embarrassed. Kids go to youth
> detention because they're bad. Not that I want them to think I'm
> bad, but I ain't telling them I'm in a shelter.

While children in the shelter are often able to make friends in their
new neighborhood or school, the embarrassment of being homeless and
in a shelter often restricts these new friendships. Additionally, children
may keep their distance from other children at school, fearing that if they
get too close, their new acquaintances will discover their shelter address.
For Tara, this involved literally forcing the children in her new school
to stay away.

> They don't know where I'm living because I never tell them. If they
> knew they'd think my mother's probably a druggie. I haven't gotten
> to know anybody at school that I like. I know a lot of people, but
> they're just too stuck up. They like me but I don't like them and
> every time they ask to play with me I just push them away.

Other children keep their distance in more subtle ways. One homeless
girl reported that she did not want children at her bus stop to know where
she lived. Each day when the bus dropped her off she told her friends
that she was only cutting through the shelter yard to get to her house, "a
big mansion with an indoor pool." Another girl used the strategy of
leaving out the word "shelter" in her address. When distributing her
address she referred only to the first words of the shelter's name, "Harbor
House," instead of "Harbor House Shelter."

Some older children do tell one or two very close friends, and hope
that they will keep it a secret. Even in these cases, it is difficult to keep
the friendship reciprocal. Friends may be accepting of the child, but not

of his or her living situation. Although Ian tries to maintain a tough facade, the pain he felt when none of his friends showed up for his fifteenth birthday party at the shelter is evident. He reported: "My friends won't visit me here either. They think it's a bum shelter. Bums! I wouldn't live with bums." He continued: "Most of them understand. But some, they're not really my friends but I see them sometimes, they don't understand." Many times, children's friends never get invited to the shelter. The homeless children themselves may prefer not to allow their peers to witness firsthand how and where they live.

Children's concerns about what would happen if their living situation were revealed are remarkably similar. They worry about being ridiculed and labelled, but most importantly, about being abandoned by their peers. Most children mention the possibility of being labelled "homeless," "bum," "alkie," "druggie," or even "homo." Nine-year-old Ingrid felt close enough to her best friend, Joanna, to bring her to the shelter; she said that Joanna only commented that "it's a real big place." Ingrid recounted:

> But I told her it's not real fun to live in a shelter because sometimes you can be there for a while. That's not so good because sometimes I like to get a house because, some of the kids in my classroom, like some of the boys, always call me names just because I live in a shelter. Sometimes they just spread it around and say, "You live in a homeless house" and stuff.

Similarly, Sean referred to the cause of his secrecy: "If kids knew I lived here . . . they'd laugh. They think it's funny because they're not living in a shelter that's why." Dana, a teenager, visualized the difficulties the revelation would cause him:

> People make fun of people who live in shelters. Because I'm the shortest kid in my grade. Well, the second shortest. They wouldn't make fun of me for being short, because some of them I could beat up. Some of the toughest kids I could beat up. They don't make fun of me. But if they know I lived in a shelter, they would spread it around. And then it would get all up to the twelfth-graders. The big twelfth-graders that I can't beat up. They would make fun of me, and I would get embarrassed and stuff. They'd say like "You live in a shelter, ha ha." And they would write on the hallway walls that I live in a shelter.

On the other hand, some children report that they do not hide their homelessness from their classmates at school. At times, the other children are accepting, as in Elizabeth's case: "Everybody knows where I live. They don't care. They'd never say anything to me about it. All my friends know. I tell them where I live. I say it's a shelter too. They say that it's fine. They really don't mind. They just care that I get into a house." Likewise, April did not hide her living situation:

A lot of my girlfriends and all of my boyfriends have been here. My friend Kami knows Christa and she knows me. She always comes over here with me. And this boy Damon and his cousin from Philadelphia always come to see me. I don't care if they know I live in a shelter.

For April, sharing that she lives in a shelter has its difficulties, such as teasing by peers, but it's still not something she wants to hide. Speaking of a boy who harasses her about it, April recounted, "this boy Carl, he said 'Ah! You live in a welfare house,' and I said 'So? It ain't no welfare house. It's a shelter.' I didn't care." She went on to tell herself: "But I got a roof over my head so I don't care. But I get mad sometimes and want to hit him."

Like April, Lisa did not choose to conceal her housing situation. She tried to appraise what homelessness means:

People at work know I live here. I mean they don't treat me any different because of it. Because I mean I'm still a person. I would expect to be treated that way, because I would treat somebody else that way. And I mean, some people at school know too. I mean I'm not just going to go out and say "Oh yeah I live in a motel" and be really happy about it because I'm not. I'm not ashamed of it and I'm not proud of it. It's just like sort of in between. And that way I mean nobody's said anything "Oh yeah you're so poor you live in a motel" or something. They just accept it.

Making New Friends

If one manages to transcend the embarrassment of being homeless, the making of new friends is also impeded by the constraints of living in a shelter or motel. Typically, childhood friendships involve inviting friends to your house to play, to celebrate a birthday, to sleep over, or, as children get older, just to hang out. Frequently, the rules of the shelter make it difficult to have friends from outside the shelter, especially if children are older and at the age where they are likely to go to friends' houses or bring friends to their house. Eight-year-old Vicky articulated this dilemma:

> What's wrong is that we have too many rules. We've got like fourteen, fifteen, twenty rules, about like curfews, and how long our phone calls would be and you can't have visitors sleep over. We can't even let our family sleep over. I'd like all my friends to sleep over. All my friends from my old house. And they can't come. Well, they can come to visit, but it wouldn't be worth it because they wouldn't be able to sleep over. Unless they slept outside, or in the closet. We can't fit anyone in the closet. It's loaded with boxes up to like the top.

Even if the friends can visit, the situation within the shelter is not always ideal for doing things with visitors. The refrigerator is not usually available for snacking. Other families are crowding the TV room, and one's own family is occupying the family's small bedroom. Staying over is almost never a possibility in a situation where there are never extra beds.

Friendships are also adversely affected by the temporary nature of one's address. In cases where children know that when they leave the shelter they will not be attending the same school, they may reason that it makes no sense to make any friends. "Why try to make friends because I'm not going to be going to that school when I get an apartment" (Eddy).

Making friends within the shelter is not that frequent an occurrence, particularly for older children. At this age, children tend to be selective about whom they choose as their friends. The small number of older children in shelters provides a very small pool from which to choose. Nine-year-old Raymond lamented: "I just have Chris to play with. There's nobody else big like me. It's good, but there's not enough big kids. I want a lot of kids if they would be nine or older than me, if they would be eleven or nine."

The relatively large numbers of preschoolers in the shelter make it more likely for younger children to find a friend. Additionally, at this age, friendship is, from a developmental perspective, a fairly superficial phenomenon. Making friends does not require great selectivity, which makes it easier to form friendships. A child is often considered a friend just by virtue of his or her proximity.

At times, close living conditions create understandable tensions between the children in the shelter. This strain can serve as a barrier to friendships. A child may perceive other children in the shelter as competitors for nurturance and other limited resources. Elizabeth, for example, felt a rivalry between herself and another girl because "they just treat this one girl, that's the same age as me, differently because she's bigger. She's just taller and she has more something. They treat her more respectfully than they treat me." This differential treatment, whether real or imagined, has created tension between the two thirteen-year-old girls.

Developing friendships in the shelter is also impeded by the relationships that develop among the adults. Whole families become friends, or whole families learn not to like each other. This often determines the patterns of the children's friendships.

The temporary nature of shelter living can impede friendships. There is a constant influx of new children and a regular loss of children who have become familiar. Older children, for whom friendships entail a significant degree of emotional involvement, may grow tired of extending themselves only to have their new acquaintances move away. Even for young children, whose friendships are more activity-based, such unstable peer relationships may cause problems. Somewhat removed from the adult world of housing plans, these young children conceptualize their friend's moves in an almost magical way. To children at this age, other people in their life seem to just "up and leave" them without notice. Children acquire a skewed view of the stability of relationships. Some even interpret the loss of friends as a personal repudiation. As one little boy who lived in a motel shared:

> This is a stupid motel! After Christmas, we're moving. I don't know where. This is a stupid motel because there ain't too much kids here. Some of my friends moved. I had one kid, Michael, one kid, Daniel, two kids moved. When they moved, I felt like I was stupid or something. They moved because those two kids didn't like me, because they wasn't even playing with me nice.

In his attempt to make sense of his friends' leaving, this child could only conclude that he himself was the cause.

In spite of these barriers to friendship, some children do manage to keep old friends or make new friends inside or outside of the shelter. In these cases, friendship can be extremely positive. It serves as a vehicle for children to share their feelings about their predicament and current living situation. After she revealed that she was homeless, Ingrid stated that her friend Joanna "talked to me a lot."

In those cases where children manage to make friends in the shelter, the friendship can be very supportive. Teddy, a five-year-old living in a motel room with his parents and two younger siblings, developed an attachment to a thirteen-year-old who lived two rooms away. He became so attached to the older boy that at points in his conversation, Teddy referred to the older boy in a knowing way as "my brother." The older boy occasionally spent some time with Teddy and helped him with his "letters and coloring." Children can provide emotional support for one another. They often tell each other about their family problems, such as the lack of money, and express their feelings openly to each other.

A number of children were able to articulate specific strategies for making friends. These skills often develop as a result of experience brought on by multiple moves. Tucker said: "I forget how I make all my friends. One friend, I remember because he was my best friend. We were on the bus and he sat on the back seat. I couldn't find a seat so I just sat with him. And then we became friends." Lisa described her experiences:

It gets uncomfortable but I'm so used to it now. It's like "Yes I'm new here," I'm not really shy anymore. I used to be really shy but you get used to it. You become more adjusting, you know. When you get into a new school you just be friendly, be courteous, just like regular things. You just try. I make friends by, I don't know how to say it but, you just be real nice to them, because I'll go up to anybody.

For many of these children, the typical childhood experiences of pain and joy surrounding friendships are intensified by being homeless. One young teenager, Sam, described his attempts to fit in with the kids at his new school. He detailed how he got a haircut because "they said to get one" and how they teased him afterward. He described how he could not afford the types of clothes most of the kids at school wore and his feeling that this contributed further to his isolation.

Such difficulties may characterize the experience of many teenagers, but the associated pain and rejection is exacerbated by many homeless children's concrete evidence that they really are different—the fact that they do not have a home. Yet for homeless children, the need for friendships is often greater than average. They need someone with whom to share the pain of their experience, to reassure them that they are okay. Thus, children like Sam are often quick to attach themselves to any accepting people whom they encounter. Sam repeatedly referred to various people, such as his social worker, social studies teacher, and shelter neighbor, as his "best friend."

Chapter Ten

"It Feels Like I'm Dumb": School

APRIL

April, age fourteen, belongs to a family of eleven girls and one boy. Only April, her brother Troy, and their sixteen-year-old sister Karyn, who is pregnant, live with their mother in the shelter. The other children are older and living on their own. Their mother is drug-involved and the family was evicted from their lifelong home after their apartment was raided by the police.

I've lived at Southfield House for three or four months. We came in February or March. It's me, my sister Karyn, my brother Troy and my mother living here. Karyn is sixteen. I'm fourteen. But we're not the only two. We got eleven girls and one boy. . . . I'm the second youngest. . . .

When I was in school before, I was at Smith Junior High. When it happened, when we got homeless, I went up to the city to my sister's for a while. I missed a week of school and my mother brought papers. Then I went to Smith Junior and then I got transferred to Burke Junior and I've been there ever since. This year I started at Smith Junior High. I didn't start in September. I started at the end of September. At the beginning of September I didn't go to school. I was in the city. Last year I went to Davenport School. I went from Davenport to the city, and I didn't go to school there. I came back here and went to Smith. I missed around three weeks of school. Now I'm at Burke. I switched when I went up to my sister's house because I kept having to pay and pay, and you know, take the bus back and forth. I still have to do that to Burke, but it's almost at the end and so I'll need to change up to Davis Junior High now. I don't know. I think I'm going to go to Burke but I don't know. I might go to Davis. My friends are everywhere. I've got friends at all schools. . . .

Living here is good I guess, I don't know. It's different than your own house. Like the pay phone, you have to pay money. And from the outside, everybody can tell it's not a regular house. It's got all these doors. But it looks like a house though. When all my friends came here, they thought it was a house. A lot of my girlfriends and all my boyfriends have been here. My friend Kami knows Christa and she knows me. She always comes over here with me. And this boy Damon and his cousin from Philadelphia always come to see me. I don't care if they know I live in a shelter. If they say something wise, I don't care. They might say "That's why you live in a shelter."

I was walking to the other part of the shelter and this boy named Carl, he said, "Ah! You live in a welfare house" and I said "So? It ain't no welfare house. It's a shelter." I didn't care. I was like "I don't live in this house anyway, I live in the one next door." He's like "Ah, you live in a welfare house" and kept laughing and rode away on his bike. But I got a roof over my head so I don't care. But I get mad sometimes and want to hit him.

I told my math teacher where I lived because she called my mother. When I'm absent or sick or something or when I don't have my homework, she'll call my mother. She called my mother and told her that I was missing some assignments. And then, she asked me where I lived and asked me "Who's Mary Margaret? She answers the phone where you live." I said "Oh this lady in the shelter." I said "She works in the shelter." My teacher said, "Oh." I only told one teacher. She said "Oh you live in a shelter. I didn't know." I said "I live on Forest Street." and she said "Where?" and I said "In a shelter." And she was like "Oh." But teachers gossip and tell each other. I don't know if she told anybody. She's got a big mouth. She always tells everything that happens. They all do. Because the people there love to talk about people. I don't know what the teachers might say if they knew, but this girl's mother said "I know how you shelter people are" when my sister Karyn and her daughter, Janine, got in an argument. She said "I know how you shelter people are, da-da da-da. Janine had a fight with a shelter girl before." My mother said "Hold on, wait a minute." She said, "Well, I'm sorry.

I didn't mean to come off the wrong way, but, it seems like the shelter people are always fighting with my daughter." I was mad she called us "shelter people." I don't know what people think about people who live in shelters. Everybody, all my friends, say "I wouldn't mind living here." The people who make fun, they think shelter people are poor! Poor like they can't get a house or something. Bums and stuff. They probably think people who live in shelters sit around the house all day or go out with their family.

If my teacher gossips I wouldn't care. But I wouldn't want her to, but she probably already did. One day my teacher said "Mrs. Jones wants to talk to you" and she asked me about my problems. She's a guidance counselor and she was asking stuff. She asked me my sisters' and brother's names. And I was telling her and she said "Well, we'll meet again" but we never met again. She gave my mother some kind of notice. She called my mother. Don't ask me why, I guess just to tell her that I went to her and stuff. My homeroom teacher said that she thinks there's a problem at home, because one day my art teacher told me to give my homeroom teacher the pass and put it on her desk and my homeroom teacher said "I don't want it. Get up here and get it." So I grabbed it and she said "Come on, we're going to the office." I said "I don't care." I went with her and the principal was at a meeting and I was staying there for the longest time, because everybody left, and she said "We'll continue this on Monday." And I said "I won't be here Monday, I have to go to court." Then she said "Oh, we'll attend to it when you come back" and I was like "Alright." The guidance counselor thought I had a lot of problems at home. And then I told her everything about home, and she said, "Well you do have problems." I don't think they're right. I got no problems. . . .

Sometimes I think teachers probably think bad of kids in shelters like, "That's why those kids are acting so bad." Then sometimes I think that they probably think shelter people are like just regular people. I don't know. . . .

When I think about being older I used to want to be what my sister was. My sister Edith used to work in the city, with computers and stuff. My sister Pat quit school and now she's going to get something classy. She's going to be what my sister Edith was. And my sister worked all her nine months when she was pregnant. She just had a baby this year. She quit because she had to take all these buses early in the morning, all different stops. But, now she works at this place where she sells clothes. It's in a store in the city. I think I want to do computers, but I'm not sure. I'm in seventh grade. I'm supposed to be in the eighth because I skipped kindergarten and just went straight to first grade. Then I went to second and they were going to keep me back in second, but they didn't. Then I went to third and then my teacher told me I was the slowest. She asked me "April, would you be mad if I kept you back?" and I said "No." I didn't care and she said, "Alright, we're going to ask your mother." My mother said she thought it's best for me to stay back, because I was a slow reader. I stayed back, and I felt bad. I wasn't mad, but I felt funny, because all my friends were past me. And I wanted to be in sixth grade because I was in fifth and they were in sixth.

Now school is good. But in one class the teacher, Miss Dowling, always gets me in trouble. Every time I talk, she say, "April, you're staying after school." She tells me every day mostly to stay after for something. And everybody else talks and she just tells them "Shut up." And she's six feet three.

I like gym and art and my friends. The hardest thing is math. History is hard too. That's Miss Dowling. Sometimes this guy Mr. Long, he talks so much. I have him first and second period. He's the electric shop guy. And he talks through the whole two periods. I hate his class. We work with kits, but there's never enough kits. I get angry. We take some classes with divorce or mental things and stuff. People from the high school and stuff come and see us. It's about mental rehab or something. And we just sit in the auditorium and talk to them all day. And then I have to sing in chorus. I miss my old school, especially my homeroom teachers. That school was hard! This one is easy. I like this one because it's easy. But I miss my teachers, gym teacher, and my homeroom teacher. They were fun. I like them.

I have to go to court May 8th. A fight happened next to my school. There was a lot of girls that beat up one girl. She's from the high school so she thought I was scared because I was junior high, but me and her started arguing and she pushed me some and spat. That's how it started. . . .

When I first started going to Burke I was shy and stuff. I was standing over on the side, but then I met my cousin there and I started having fun. At first I felt sad because I had to go there. I was mad. I was crying when I first had to leave Smith. This lady went to pick me up, because I had gone to my sister's and she had to pick me up and brought me over my mother's on Market Street. And my mother was with her daughters and one of my sister's boyfriends. . . . Yup, that was the day of my birthday, I got kicked out. I had to move out of Smith. It was a sad birthday. But then my sisters had a party for me. I was late for my own birthday. Everybody was there waiting for me. And my sisters, I was supposed to leave early and my sister was like "April when are you coming? When you coming?" and my sister Kim over here was saying "We're having a surprise party for you." She told me. I was like "Alright" and then we didn't end up going until about nine o'clock and got there by ten-thirty and I was mad. Because everybody was getting ready to leave, but then I felt cheap because everybody was singing happy birthday to me. And had a big cake they made me, a lot of ice cream, and all that stuff.

TUCKER

Nine-year-old Tucker and his sister Bethany, whose story was presented earlier, came to the shelter three days ago with their mother. They have been in many shelters in the past. Most recently they were living with their maternal grandmother.

I'm nine. I live here. I don't know when I came here. I think two days ago. When my mom said we were going to come here I didn't think it would be very fun. I thought it was going to be like when we went to a shelter before and we didn't have peace. We didn't have quiet, no equal rights, but this place is different. I don't remember much about the last shelter. All I remember was I didn't like it. We used to sleep on cots and that's about all I remember. And we never used to have equal rights. It was always like "man I can't wait to get out." No equal rights is like You can't do anything. You can't even play. All the rooms there was for beds. There was no playroom. That's what was bad there. We kind of didn't have equal rights there. They told you when you had to go to bed, told you when you had to wake up, and they told you everything. They told you when you had to be back at the shelter if you went out. I forget. It was a long time ago. I was small. Then I told my mother I didn't like it and she moved out. She didn't like it either.

When I first came here it was pretty boring because I didn't know you could play after supper and everything. We didn't know where the playroom was so when we had supper we just went into the room we went into at nighttime and we went to sleep. We didn't know where the playroom was. . . .

I try to help my mom. Sometimes when we get things that my mother doesn't get, like ice cream, I always give her more than all the other kids. My sister, Bethany, gives her only a little bit. And I'm like "Here have a lot." I gave her one big bite of it at the beginning and at the end I give her a big bite. The others don't give much because they're stingy! And I'm not.

When I heard we had to leave our house again, I didn't like it. We move a lot. A lot! Once my mother moves she says "Alright, this is different. I'm going to like this place." Then she don't like it, so she moves to another place. Then she don't like that anymore. She doesn't even like my own grandmother's. I don't know why. She just has her reasons to move. I don't remember if she ever tells us what they are. We move so much, man. Once I said "I want to move from here," because I had no friends there and nobody was polite. Everybody just wanted to fight. I wanted to get out of there, man. I wanted friends. The last place was Rhode Island. I had a couple friends there, and I had a fight there, too. But that was the only thing. But then that's when my grandmother kicked us out. Then that's when we had to come to live here.

It's hard to make friends every time you move. I used to have a girlfriend, well kind of like a girlfriend, and we moved, man, and I was like heartbroken, man. I used to have friends that are boys too. I didn't think about leaving them as much as I think about leaving my girlfriend. Moving all the time makes it tough getting to school that much. Once I settle down in one school, we have to go to another school. We have to get the transport papers, and put them in another school and something wrong happens every time! Like one time they didn't know I had special needs so they had to put me in another school because they had special needs. Then we had to take all those transport papers, put them in the other school, and then there was no problem there! I was in there for two days and that's when my grandmother kicked us out. Now we have to take the transport papers from there, bring them to here, from Rhode Island to whatever state this is. Then we have to bring it to the school. Then we're probably going to have another problem. I don't like it when that happens. It feels like "I'm dumb" man. Because a lot of the kids that are in school are learning things and when I get into school it's like, I can't do all the work they're doing because I'm out of school so long. And I can't do the work they're doing. I have to catch up more. It feels like I'm dumb. I don't think I'm dumb. It's just that I wasn't in school. But some people might call me dumb. Some people might call me dumb sometimes, because I can't do the work they do. I tell them but, man, they don't listen to that. I guess I'm going to have to show them they can't mess around with me. I'll give them a black eye. I never actually gave anybody a black eye, yet. I feel like it, though.

In school I'm special needs. That means you need more help than the other kids. You're a little slow. That means that you don't learn that fast. They told me in school I need special needs. My mother and the school teacher was talking. She said "He needs special needs" and all this stuff.

"We don't provide special needs in this school so he's going to have to go to another school." I don't know how many schools I've been in. My mother knows. It's been a lot. In the first grade one school. Second grade was two schools. Third grade was two schools. Well, second grade and third grade were the same school for part. And I stayed back in kindergarten. In kindergarten it was the same school. Two different kindergartens, not two different schools. Now I'm in third grade. I'm.a smart kid. . . .

I'd like a house. I don't know why other people are here, but I guess it's because they don't have any money to buy a house or an apartment either. Some kids never have to come here because their mothers are rich probably. Some mothers are smart, some mothers are dumb. Some mothers work, some mothers don't. Some mothers get good jobs, some mothers don't. My mom can't get a job because she thinks this way: she's got three kids and she's not going to work because she don't trust us with anybody. I think she's right, because I seen a show that's true. It's called "911." Once it talked about this girl that went to work and the kids got abused by the babysitter. And that's why I think that my mother has the right idea. Coming here to a shelter is better than something bad happening, like being abused. On the TV show the kid called 911 and 911 came over. I think their baby-sitter hit them a lot. She hit them. There was this little baby, and it hurt man. I could just feel it. It never happened to me. When we used to get in trouble, we used to get sent into the room, not hit. . . .

I miss my friends. When we moved I had to not be friends anymore with my old friend. But we bought this used car, for one hundred dollars, and then I could go over my friend's house. My mother could drive me there and we could play. It was one year before I saw him. Then it was alright, because we finally could see each other and we could play again. He had all these new friends that I didn't know how he became friends with them. I went there a couple times until my mother sold the car! Stupid. And then, I couldn't see him anymore. She sold the car because she needed money. Sometimes I get mad about moving so much. Sometimes I say "Ma, why we have to move?" She says "Because I wanted to." I don't think it's a very good answer, but she's the mother. You have to do what she says.

If other kids needed to know about this place, I'd tell them that it's nice. And if they're ever poor this is the place. If they ever get poor or they run away, this is the place. Being poor is not having much money. You don't have enough money to move, so they have these places, like this shelter, for people to move. It's a good idea to have these places.

I can make money sometimes. I got four pennies here to give to some place where people donate things. I have it in my jacket. They donate in the center where we stay during the day. It helps. It's better than no pennies. I thought I should donate more, but I don't have enough money to donate more because I'm not rich. I just want to say one thing. If I'm ever rich, I might donate a lot of money to the poor, because I know how it is to be poor. If I'm ever rich, I'll just donate and donate every day. I wouldn't buy things for myself. I'd donate my money. Lots of it. They use it to buy food for the poor. In other countries they don't have anything. My grandmother lived there once and she didn't like it. She didn't like to see all those kids starving and everything. She said one was holding on to my grandad "Bring me home with you, bring me home with you." I wouldn't like that either. I don't know what country she saw that in.

If I told teachers and other grown-ups what it's like for a kid to be homeless, I would say that it's not very good. I'd tell them that if they're rich they should help a lot. They're nice people but they might think "If I donate too much money the poor people might get rich." Some people are so rich and they don't donate money. But people should donate money.

COMMENTARY

In their different ways, April and Tucker describe, in considerable detail, their history of schooling. For both of these children, school is a struggle. They are like many homeless children who have attended multiple schools and find themselves unable to catch up. They are trying valiantly to stay engaged, but seem to be at serious risk for becoming dropouts.

A significant amount has been written about the education of children who are homeless (Rafferty and Rollins, 1989). School systems, especially in large urban settings, have considerable difficulty adjusting and responding to the needs of these children. Yet, while we know many statistics about the reading scores, attendance, grade retention, and dropout records for these children, we know very little about how school is experienced by these children. Certainly, the statistics are critical to advocacy and the general improvement of conditions. However, the perspective of the individual child is critical to any teacher, parent, or social worker who is trying to respond to the particular needs of a homeless child. For children who are homeless, the school provides a mixture of positive and negative experiences.

Enjoying School

For some children, particularly in the early grades, school can be a place that is steady, secure, and safe. It may serve as a place where children can be relatively free of worry, develop bonds with caring teachers, and develop their own strengths and interests. In a world that often demands that they endure and respond as adults, school allows them to be children. For many, it serves as a distraction from the worrisome and emotionally charged events of their lives in the shelter as it absorbs their energy for a significant amount of time each day. It also provides them with a predictable routine and set of consequences, unlike the more chaotic circumstances of the shelter. If the learning environment is positive, they are able to feel a sense of competence as they master new skills.

At the interpersonal level, school provides an environment in which they can form positive relationships with other children and make new friends. Some children develop strong and positive attachments to teachers or school support staff. Seventeen-year-old Barbara, who had a history of unstable living conditions, abuse, and family violence, vividly remembered the support of her first grade teacher. "I like everything about her. She was so nice. Still to this day I see her, I go to see her. . . . Because I think she really believed what I was telling her."

School may also provide children with a chance for some enjoyable diversions from the worries of their everyday life. Maggie expressed her enthusiasm for school in terms of the pleasure she experienced doing "drama." "Last Thursday I was the farmer's wife in the fifth room and everybody had two parts, some had three. And Monday we're going to do a puppet show." Juan became engaged in school because he viewed it as a means of breaking out of his current situation. He described his efforts to study hard. This was part of his plan to earn a scholarship to a prestigious local academy, from which he would continue on to Harvard.

Changing Schools

On the other hand, having to change schools frequently and begin all over in so many different places can make school a negative experience for many children. Negative associations regarding school appear to be more prominent for older homeless children. The concrete comforts of school that a younger child might note, such as a favorite food, story, or book, are not present for older children, who are more in tune to the threats to their self-esteem inherent in the school experience.

Homelessness often means living in many geographic settings over the course of a few months or years. If the move is within a limited distance, some children manage to stay in the same school. If the move is a more distant one, the result is a change of schools. In spite of the McKinney law, which gives children the right to remain in the same school until the end of the school year, most families and children choose to transfer schools. This is often due to lack of knowledge about their legal rights. Others find transportation difficult. Children sometimes choose to transfer schools in an attempt to hide their embarrassment at becoming homeless.

The constant moving from one school to another is particularly distasteful to children. It is difficult both socially and academically. Many older children, particularly those from families with a history of frequent moves, have attended a long string of schools. For some of these adolescents, a history of thirteen or fourteen schools is not unusual. Because their school experience is so significant for them, children usually can present quite an accurate account of all these schools, recalling each school grade by grade. Dana, who is fourteen, described the list of schools he has attended:

> Kindergarten I went over my grandmother's. I forget the name of the school. It's on the corner of Brill and Second Street, but I forget the name of it. I went there all the way up to second grade. And then from second grade I went to Taylor and Arbor Park. I went there 'til fourth grade, then after fourth grade I went to another school. I forget the name of it. I forget the name of the street. Downey School. I went to that school 'til fifth grade, then when I got out of the fifth I moved to Fairhale and I started going to Creamer Junior High School all the way to eighth. And then I go to Fairhale High School.

For children who have developed relationships with teachers and peers, these moves are very painful. This is particularly true for adolescents, for whom the peer group is becoming an increasingly important element of their identity. Lisa reported: "I've been to twelve schools counting this one. I don't like it, because you get real close to somebody and all of a sudden it's like boom, you got to go and you get really uncomfortable around meeting new people. 'Oh that's the new girl.' That's how it is."

Some children plan elaborate ways to avoid this loss. Dana, anticipating another new start since coming to the shelter stated:

I want to go finish at my old school. I want to. I have to get up at like four o'clock in the morning to get the train back and forth. I'll take the train there and then when I get out of school, I'll walk around to my father's house. My old school's right around the corner from my old house. And then I'll wait till he gets off work so he can bring me back home to the shelter.

Being the New Kid

A new school means establishing new relationships, making new friends among the students, and establishing new alliances with teachers and administrators. It means walking into the building on your first day, usually in the middle of the year, and presenting yourself to the school administrators, usually the principal and guidance counselors. For most children and adolescents, this event is particularly awkward because they are required to list their address on the application forms. This address will probably reveal that they live in a shelter for the homeless, a fact they are desperately trying to hide. Many children walk into a new school alone, since their mothers are busy at the shelter, filling out welfare forms and watching their younger siblings.

Meeting new friends is also difficult for these children. Even under ordinary circumstances, moving to a new school in the middle of the school year challenges the interpersonal skills of most children. Doing this repeatedly grade after grade leaves a child feeling on the fringe, on the outside looking in. But when a child is homeless, the task is even more formidable. A child is not just the "new kid," but the "homeless kid," and carries with him or her all the stigma that the label implies. Troy described his difficulty being accepted: "I got a C in gym. I just couldn't play the games like, because people used to laugh at me every time I messed up. I just couldn't. I would just always sit out at gym because kids were making fun if I did something wrong. They call me a loser and stuff."

As many of these children find themselves getting comfortable in their new school environment, they discover that it's time to move again. As Ryan stated: "I've been in four schools this year. It's rough. Always having to move and change and get used to people and make new friends. It takes a little while. And right when I get it, then right when I get friends and get used to stuff, then we have to move again." This is a common story for the homeless child, since shelter living is, by definition, temporary. When housing is finally found, children have to move schools again. For some, this thought is so painful that they find themselves wishing that they could stay in the shelter. Alison, age twelve, was getting her new apartment the next day. Although excited, she also faced the move with some trepidation: "I won't be glad to leave here. No, because I may be nervous when I go to Kennedy School because I'm already used to this school and I'm anxious to see the apartment, to move in but, I don't want to leave this school."

Keeping Homelessness a Secret

Many homeless children spend a considerable amount of energy hiding their homelessness from teachers. Children's reasons for keeping their situation a secret are related to the embarrassment they anticipate experiencing. Some believe that, while their teacher could be trusted not to embarrass them with the information, she might tell other teachers. This would result in the word getting out eventually to the other children. Others are worried that the teacher would not like them if he or she knew that they were living in a shelter. These children assume that their perceptions of homeless people as "druggies and bums" are shared by their teachers. Tara expressed her feelings about the fact that her teacher knows she lives in a shelter: "She's supposed to know those things. I don't think she likes it too much, because she's always, always yelling at me. She yells at me more than other kids. She yells at me for nothing. She yells at me a lot just because I'm in a shelter!"

For the few children who manage to remain in the same school they attended prior to coming to the shelter, there is also a significant worry. These children are often terrified that their teacher will find out that they no longer live in the same school district. Such exposure will lead them to be transferred to another school. Isabella, while attributing benevolent feelings to her teacher, expressed a reluctance for her to find out where she lives: "If I told her I was homeless, I think she'd feel sorry. And she'd say 'Why didn't you tell me before?' and I don't want to tell her because then I'll have to go to another school and I don't want to go to another school because I already have friends."

Gaps in Learning

Changing school presents problems not only in terms of social interaction but also in terms of academic progress. Homeless children experience significant gaps in their learning and are always in the position of trying to catch up. These gaps are the consequences of a number of different factors, which work together to make school learning a very difficult chore. The variation in school curricula across schools, school districts, and states is a major contributor to homeless children's uneven pattern of learning. Academic skills, such as beginning reading and problem solving, are taught at different rates and using different teaching methods. One school district may teach beginning reading using a phonics method, while another may use a sight method. One classroom moves more quickly through problem solving skills than another. School districts use any of a number of reading series, with marked differences to which new children must adjust. Some skills may never be taught to these children, while other skills may be taught two or three times. Stephanie lamented: "It's not very good living in all these places. It's hard because at school, in Texas, they were in times tables and up here they were just learning times tables. The schools are doing different things."

Gaps in learning also result from the frequent absences that characterize the school attendance of homeless children. A move into or out of a shelter can be costly to a child's school time. Homelessness often comes suddenly, leaving the family little opportunity for an organized move. Transferring into a new school means acquiring records from the old school. Mothers overwhelmed with the details of trying to find shelter for their families, or unfamiliar with the ways of schools, are often not aware of the necessity to gather records from the child's previous schools. Different school districts have different requirements for entrance.

In addition to records, a new school may require updated immunizations or a medical examination, which means the family must locate and schedule an appointment with a physician. In the process, days and weeks may go by with the child just hanging around the shelter waiting to get into school. Some moves are made near the end of the school year or approaching a school vacation. Families often see little point in starting the children for the few remaining days or weeks. As a consequence, homeless children can lose significant time in school, adding to the gaps in learning that they already experience. Ian stated: "I hate school so bad. I just made it this year. I had forty absences all year. I was absent so much because we were moving around so much."

Another source of the child's uneven pattern of learning is the limited attention that many of these children are able to give to school. Many are worried and preoccupied about what is happening to their mothers and siblings back at the shelter, or about when they are going to find a permanent home. These children spend a fair amount of school time staring out the window, as one child put it, "just worrying, worrying about just everything." Learning the names of state capitals seems, at that moment, to have less significance than trying to figure out what city or state one will be living in this time next year.

The reinforcement of learning that is provided by homework, or at least by the encouragement of parents, is often missing for these children. Completing homework assignments is not easy in the shelter. The noise level is often high, and finding a quiet place to work is difficult. As one teenager noted: "It's hard to do your homework. It's noisy. You got these little kids running around screaming like that." Lisa shares a motel room with her family. For both Lisa and her mother, who is attending college classes, doing homework is a challenge:

> I used to be really good at school, and I still could be if I wanted to, I just don't try as much because it's harder to study. People here are constantly asking questions, "Where's this? Where's that?" and I know my mom has the same problem. And everybody's bugging you when you do your homework.

Shelters do not have the luxury of study halls. The top of the bed is the "desk," with two or three siblings playing in the same room. Moreover, parents may not have the luxury of a sufficient supply of emotional energy to invest heavily in their child's school progress. Moms are trying to survive in the shelter and figure out how to find permanent housing. The child's math papers often take a back seat to filling out welfare forms.

As a result of the gaps in learning, many homeless children constantly feel that they are behind, that they are never caught up to their classmates. Learning the more advanced skills presumes that children have learned the more basic skills. Children with major deficits in their earlier learning are building on a house of cards. Their grasp on the subject matter is never more than tenuous. The further they progress in school, the wider the gap becomes. As children move into middle and high school, they often feel hopeless about their chance of ever being on the same plane as the other students. The risk of dropping out becomes very high.

Special Needs

While moving from school to school is difficult for children who have no intrinsic learning problems, it is severely complicated for children who have learning disabilities of any kind. Children with specific learning disabilities, children who may be slow learners, or children with emotional or behavioral problems require individualized educational services and are legally entitled to these services. These children must have extensive evaluations before the appropriate service plan can be decided upon and implemented.

Moving from one school to another almost always results in a disruption of the evaluation process or the delivery of services. Old records are sometimes lost or are significantly delayed in delivery. Children are often reevaluated in the new school, and must adjust to new educational programs. Both the evaluation of the child's learning needs and the implementation of the plan take considerable time, particularly in large, overburdened urban districts. Parents, who often know little about the intricacies of the law, or the precise nature of their children's problems, are usually unable to serve as effective advocates for their children. For many of these children, continuous moving results in falling further behind and, for a good number, falling permanently between the cracks.

Consequences of Disrupted School Experience

As a result of the disrupted school experience and the many shifts in schools they undergo, homeless children, particularly as they get older, often end up feeling socially isolated. The frequent leaving of friends, and the difficulty of breaking into new circles and making new friends, often results in their feeling alone and disconnected. They have no group to whom they belong; adolescents, in a desperate effort to belong, often join a fringe group. At one level, Ian overtly prided himself on being a member of a small group of "freaky skateboarders." At another level he was significantly saddened because most kids at school didn't like him. He hated going to school and could not wait to get out.

Academically, homeless children are on the fringe. Their inadequacies leave them feeling "dumb and stupid." While they are aware on the one hand that external circumstances may have caused their school problems, on the other hand they are not sure that they are not personally responsible for the school failure they experience. In Tara's case, "I stayed back in second grade because my grandmother died and I didn't do anything. I missed her, that's why I did all the stuff. I misbehaved."

Despairing at their current situation, some homeless adolescents come to conclude that school learning is irrelevant. Since it does not help them solve the immediate issues of their homelessness and family problems, and since they are failing its requirements, school appears to them to have no value. Ian, whose family and social struggles had been going on for years, came to the conclusion that you "don't need to know about neutrons to buy a donut!" These children often arrive at the point where they hate school and look forward to the day when they can "just get out."

Occasionally children can recover, particularly if they move to a school where expectations are high. Dana, whose move to the shelter involved leaving the city for a more suburban area, reported that he once felt this way, but has since changed his mind:

> I'd never do my homework. Other kids up there, they give you influence. They're like "you're doing your homework? Oh man, you sucker!" And so, like every day when I used to start to do my homework, people used to keep telling me "Oh man, why you doing your homework?" I'd be like "I don't know. What am I doing my homework for?" and I would throw it away. And so, out here, people got the attitude that you're going to be somebody. So I just follow the people, my friends' footsteps. And then I just started doing my homework and I just started getting A's and B's.

Chapter Eleven

"We Manage but It Isn't Easy": Coping

VICKY

Vicky came to the shelter with her mother ten days ago, after they had spent three days in a motel. Prior to this she was living with her maternal grandmother, while her mother was in an alcohol rehabilitation facility. Her mother is currently pregnant and they are in the shelter trying to get a certificate for subsidized housing. Vicky's parents met while in college and divorced when she was a preschooler. She sees her father occasionally.

I'm eight years old and I'm going into fourth grade. I'm young for fourth grade. I started in nursery school when I was three. I was five, that was kindergarten, six was first, seven was second, third was eight and now I'll be in fourth and I'll be nine. Other kids are around like ten and eleven. I do good in school. My last report card got almost all excellents. I'm reading *Little House on the Prairie* for the summer. It's a hard book for fourth grade but it's easy to me because the teacher read most of it before we got out of school, so I know what the words are in case I need some help. She started it in the middle of the year but she couldn't finish the book because it was thick. It was a hard cover, but I took the soft cover. I went to Joseph P. Westwood school this year. That's in Burham. My grandparents live there. I was living with them. After school got out, I came down here. It's a long way. On the way down to here there's a McDonald's and we meet my mom on the side going up to the shore. Then I go home the rest of the way in my mom's car.

My grandfather is a scientist. I stayed with my mom's mom and my mom's dad all winter. I went to third grade there. I went to second and first grade in Burham too. Before my mother went to the alcoholic place, we used to live there. My mother and I had an apartment. But we just moved there five years. That was in the city. First, when I was borned, I lived in the city. And then I moved to Burham. We moved to Burham when I was six. First I was in the hospital, then I moved to King Street, then to Sherville, which was Belmont Street, then I moved to Independence Way I think in Burham. Then I moved to Chesterfield Drive in Burham. Then I moved to Berry Way and now I'm at Harbor House. I moved a lot of times. This will be my eighth time moving when we get out of the shelter. And I'm eight years old. That's a lot of moves. One a year. . . .

So I stayed with my grandmother all through third grade and since I got out of school I moved out here so I could be with my mom and so she could go on welfare. So, after I got out of school, the day after, because my mom was busy the day before, I came out here with my two friends because I wanted to have some friends in the car. And I also wanted to say goodbye to them because they're my best friends. . . .

Moving is kind of fun, sort of. The big move when we move into a house, it's going to be so fun, because it's going to be like having a huge Christmas, because the whole garage is full. Our stuff is in my grandmother's garage because we couldn't put it in storage because it was too expensive. All our furniture is in my grandmother's garage. And in my grandfather's work room, which is a place on the other side of the garage. And the porch downstairs which is so loaded we can hardly walk in it and in my bedroom, which is where my desk is and the TV, we got two TV's. I keep one in my room at my grandmother's and the den which is downstairs. And when we make the big move, we're going to have to unload all the boxes inside and I'll be saying "Oh I forgot about this!" Last June, nine months ago, me and my mom put all our furniture at my grandmother's and I stayed with my grandmother and my mother went to AHR. That's a place for people who drink too much. And before that, I almost forgot, another place. I had to move to my grandmother's twice because my mom went somewhere else too because she had a problem with drinking and driving and stuff.

We lived a normal life until she was twenty-nine. I was born when she was twenty-two. Then when she was twenty-nine, she started drinking and I was kind of worried. So a long time ago, she was in the first place for a month and then she came back. Then it was normal for a while again. Then last June, she had to go to AHR which was a program for two weeks to a month before she got to Cooleridge House for alcoholics. Then she went to Cooleridge House for five months. And I stayed with my grandmother.

Well, in between AHR and Cooleridge House she was home for one night. That's when we went to the movies. And she had a blackout at the movies. No, she didn't have it at the movies, she had it when she came back home. She forgot where she put her money because she found a lot of money that day. I think it was from her paycheck. She got the blackout because she drank too much. It was the drink. Because she used to put vodka in her coke and in her orange juice and in her coffee and her apple juice. And her orange pineapple juice. And sometimes she drank it straight without a drink and I hated it.

Once we went to a beach where we could go swimming. My mother bought coke, but she brought a little container of vodka and she poured vodka in there. I said "Ma, do you always have to do that? Sometimes I might want to take a drink but I can't because it's got some alcohol in it." I didn't say it to her, but I was thinking "Ma! Quit it! That's bad." My grandmother knew. And my grandfather knew but my father didn't. He knew after she went to Cooleridge House, otherwise he thought she was just drinking for fun.

It happened after they were divorced. I know why she was drinking. She had a problem. Like I figured that out myself. My grandmother helped me to figure it out a little but I did most of it. I talked to my grandmother. I was able to call her on my mom's phone. And soon I might be getting my own phone and get a number so I can talk alone because my baby sister or brother, could just scramble in and I'd say "Back off. Out, out, out." I might be getting a lock on my door. I'm getting a new baby sister, in December. My mom's having a baby. Hopefully it's a girl. I don't know what I want, a boy or a girl. If it's a boy I get my own bedroom. If it's a girl I'd share a bedroom but I'd have a girl to play with. I've had some bad stuff happen to me but I do a lot of thinking and figuring out. My grandmother helped me the most.

I'm worried about the new baby coming. My mom's been drinking a lot of coffee and she's not supposed to drink much and she's been smoking a lot. That could affect on the baby. She told me. She's not smoking tons, though. It's a little less than usual. She usually smokes almost every hour. But yesterday, she had to smoke every four hours because of the circus. We went to the circus and she was smoking there but not as much because we were busy seeing things. I'm not even ever going to start smoking.

But maybe nothing will happen to the new baby. My mom smoked when she had me. I was oversize. I was okay. I was oversized when I was born. All the other kids were like one foot three and I was twenty-two inches. I was almost two feet. I weighed nine pounds, five ounces. I was a big baby. So far I'm my mom's only child. Getting a new baby's going to be different. . . .

We came to this shelter because we didn't have a place to go. We signed up because we couldn't go on welfare on our own because we needed some help to find things we can get. My mom didn't know we could get three hundred dollars for the baby and we can get it now. And we will be able to get thirty-five dollars worth of free food at the supermarket. My mom just started to apply for welfare when she was almost at court and then we got in here because someone mentioned it. It's going to help us being in here. The people who work here help us find things, they help us fight for stuff and they help us get stuff and they can tell us what we can get. Welfare doesn't want to give it all to us, but the people here already know all of it so they can give it to them and so we get more stuff on welfare.

We have to be here in the shelter until we get our certificate. The certificate is for a house. It will take around six months. Some people stayed here for six months before they got it. It's going to be kind of fun because I can make a lot of friends. But I'll also be kind of sad, because I won't get all my stuff and all my stuffed animals which I've got three trash bags full. They're all down in Burham. Except for three of them. I have Snuggles, Charley Bear, and Little Joe. I can't wait to get my mom's big, humongous teddy bear. It's about five feet high. Both me and my mom like stuffed animals. She needs it to lean on so she won't fall over, like, badoom and squish the new baby. So she needs Charley Bear to lean on. I need to hug them and also, I feel safer with them. And also we heard the security guard here yell last night, so we know that he works. He said, "Hold it right there." Well, I saw him because my mom came home exactly at eleven o'clock. I wasn't alone. I was with Paula. Sometimes I worry here. They could just climb over the fence because it's not that high. I can even climb it. We can lock the doors but we can't lock the windows and also they leave the windows open so we can get some fresh air and they can just slip through the screens. I didn't worry about this at my grandmother's. No! Because we were upstairs! Here it might not be that safe. Also I got to sleep in my grandmother's room all the time because my bedroom was always stuffed and all the clothes were on my bed. Once I was so scared because she wasn't there and I crawled into my bed, which had stuff all around it, which would take a million years to get through it and I was hiding. And I even had the big pillow around me so nothing could get to me. Sometimes I get scared at night. I don't get bad nightmares but my mom does.

I don't know how I think about the new baby. They'll be almost a ten years difference. I rounded it off. For school in the fall I don't know where I'll be yet. Not Burham. Definitely around here. It's going to be fun because I'm going to make new friends. My old friends I can keep. Once in a while, when I go down to visit my grandmother, I can see them. I already did once, but I can't visit her for three weeks since Thursday. She went up to see her other grandchildren in Oregon. I like to see my friends when I visit there. I definitely will make some new friends here. Because in first grade I didn't know any and just the second day I was like, "Wow, wow, I've got thirteen friends!" And when I was in nursery school, my mom thought that I was going to be like "Mom, don't leave me." But I was like "Bye Mom, leave, I'm fine. Hey, wanna play with me? Shoo, bye Mom. Go go. Go bye bye." I figured out how to make friends. It's easy. Just be nice to them and ask them what their name is and play with them.

Probably when I go to school I'll be living here. Well maybe, I don't know. My friends in Burham know I'm here because I gave some of them my address. They don't know what this place is. Not yet. I might tell them. I don't tell them I live in a shelter, but I call it Harbor House. And I put Little Harbor Road, #10, Harbor House, Wanconset. I don't know the zip code, Unit 8. Sometimes I tell them it's a shelter. I don't know why only sometimes. It's embarrassing. Maybe a lot of kids feel the same. They like it here but they don't like telling people that it's a shelter so they just call it Harbor House. . . .

I don't know what my new house is going to be like. Empty, I guess, because we won't have anything in it yet. Then we get our furniture from Burham. And it will be full!

The dad for the new baby is named Kevin Durant and my mother might get married to him. He does not live in this town, but in another one. He has two jobs. And he rents a place that's right near the beach, even closer. All you do is go out the house, down the path to the beach! And we could use his big house. There's six people. He's divorced, too and he has three kids and my mom has one kid, me, and soon it will be five kids if they get married and then it will be them two so it will be seven people in the family. It would be good if she got married because she could have a father helping to take care of the baby. But it will also be kind of bad because then we'd have to go off welfare because he has a job. We won't get food stamps and then she'll have to go out of school, because she's going to go to Junior

College now. She wants to stay in college because she didn't finish when she was in college. She dropped out, don't ask me why. It was getting kind of hard. She went to Bickford College I think. Same with my dad. He dropped out too. I'm hoping to go to Harvard and then I'm going to go to medical school. I'll be the first woman doctor in our family. The idea just came out of my head. Nobody told me. I want there to be a doctor in the family. My grandfather is a scientist. He went to Harvard or Yale. I want to become a bone doctor. . . .

You can try and go on welfare alone but it's tough because you don't get it, but you can. You need to have kids I think. And also you have to quit the job but the kids can still work and they can make money and it doesn't count. They can just play with it or spend it on extra things like circus tickets. I might be babysitting when I'm ten, maybe even nights. Maybe they need it here at the shelter. I can only have one customer at a time. That's all I need, fifty cents an hour. First I got to check it out with my mom. And then with the office! Then I'll ask Mary, so I can help out at the children's center so I know what to do in case anything happens. And I'll be a little agency. But it will be kind of hard if there's two kids sick. Yuck. I want to do it. I want to babysit. First I'll check it out with my mom, then I'll check out with the office, then I'll check out with Miss Mary. . . .

School is good. When we went to that pool for the first time I passed the deep water test, so I was able to jump off the diving board without a lifeguard and swimming lessons. And I jumped off the board and I peddled, then I turned myself upside down, but I was in the water and I swam down to the bottom, did a handstand and bounced up! When I get a little heavier I could just do a pencil. I love to go swimming. Once I get in the water it's like "Oh there's a rest period already! I just got in!"

My teacher in school is good. She was nice. And I'm lucky because she helped me with everything. Well, she called me up several times and talked to me and she said, "If there's anything you need, just talk to me." I didn't even have to go up there and talk to her. She knew it was hard. I'll miss that school. . . .

My mom never spanks me. I do what she tells me. I don't know what would happen if I didn't because I always do it. Sometimes my mom makes me mad. I tell her kind of.

T. J.

T. J., age seventeen, is currently in the twelfth grade and is the oldest in a family of six children. The stories of his sisters, Ingrid and Elizabeth, were presented earlier. They have been in the shelter for five months and have not lived in a shelter before. Living on AFDC benefits only, their mother became overwhelmed by bills and fell behind in rent payments.

I'm seventeen years old I'm a senior in high school. I came here a few months ago. My mom has been here longer. Before that I lived with my aunt and before that I was living with my mother. I don't really know what happened. I think it just got so hard for my mother. I don't know. She had to work every day, come home with six kids. It just got hard for all of us. It would have been hard for me trying to do that. Money was tight too. She tried, and I'm not saying she did a bad job or anything, she didn't. She did the best she could. She tried to do what was best. Coming here was best for all of us, because, I guess, she wants help. I'm not trying to say she needs help, but, I don't know how to explain it. Like rent, plus food and things, that was hard. That would mean she would have to work hard longer. And after a while, I guess it got hard. We always had food but it was hard.

When I heard we were coming here to the shelter, at first I didn't want to come. When I think of a shelter, I think like a big room with cots and things, not something like this. The word shelter, I thought of the shelters up in the city, for all the people on the streets and stuff. My mother said, it wasn't like that. She thought it would be better, too, if I went with my aunt, because there's no guys here. And, she just thought it would be better. I went to my aunt's for the summer. I have a cousin that's my age too. That was fine. When I came here I felt alright. I wasn't mad or anything about coming here. We're leaving soon. I haven't seen my new house. I just haven't gone over there any time my mother has gone. I know it's a nice house.

The hardest part living here is probably, the way I am. I'm so set in the ways I do things. Like I'm not conscious of other people sometimes. There's just so many people. They're all ladies too. That's another thing. It's different with men and ladies, because ladies are different, have different attitudes than men do I guess. I won't say high strung. Let's see, they're just, I don't know what it is. It's just different from my sisters. I'm used to my sisters and the way they are and they are used to me, but when you come here different people have different ways, it's hard to explain. I mean nothing's really hard for me to do. It's just stuff I don't like. Since I'm seventeen they give me more freedom than the little kids. And so there's not a lot put on me. I know I have an attitude problem, but that's just the way I am and I always probably will be. I probably get upset so easily. It's just different here. It's like having a bunch of little sisters, that's what it is. But there's a lot of older ladies too and they still feel like little sisters. And, sometimes they'll get on your nerves. Sometimes they're nice. And there's babies here too. Crying babies. I don't mind that much, but when they're crying constantly, like my brother and sister do. But, that don't get me upset until I get crazy. It's not bad. To get away I usually go into my room and just listen to the radio, my tapes. I have a room to myself. . . .

In school I usually describe the shelter as an apartment house to the other kids. I just use that. It isn't a lie. It is a house. Five of my friends know I live here. They don't know it's a shelter. It's embarrassing. Not embarrassing but I don't like using the word shelter really. It's kind of embarrassing. When they ask questions I try to avoid them and avoid the questions and stuff. I don't like to get too in depth into the question. I can't explain why it's embarrassing. It's just when you say homeless you probably refer to people sleeping on the streets. That's what I think. But when you really think about homeless, it only means when you don't have a house that's in your name. It's like being in between houses. That's how I think about it. In between houses. I don't know what other kids think. I don't really know how they think about that. They never talk about it. So I just say I'm living in an apartment house. . . .

What I like here is that I don't have to watch kids all the time. Where we lived before, I had to watch them while my mother went to work. And, I get a little more freedom here than I used to have. But I'm older now. It would probably be the same way if we didn't come here. I would have probably still had the same freedom as I do now, with my mother. She treats me pretty responsibly. Right now I could probably raise the kids by myself if I had the money because I just know how to raise kids. I don't want to though! I don't want any kids. I don't even want to wait a while. I don't want any! Period. No. No. I don't want to get married either. I just don't want to.

I see my dad every week. He lives in East Seton. He's mine, Ingrid's, Beth's, and Chris' dad. My mom and dad broke up then got back together. It wasn't hard when they broke up. I can't remember how old I was when they first broke up. They were separated for about a month, so I was about six or seven maybe. I can't remember when they first did. When they got back together and then left again really it didn't bother me. I don't know why, it just didn't. At first I didn't want them to get back together because they fought sometimes and I didn't want to see my mother go through it again. So for me it was okay when they broke up. But after a while we wanted them together. At first I didn't want it, because I didn't want to see them fighting. But after a while I got used to it. Then he left again and they broke up again. It's harder on the little kids than it would probably be on me. We manage, but it isn't easy.

I don't know really what to say about living here. There's nothing wrong with it. But it's different than a house. . . . And like I say to myself "This is my house" instead of saying "I don't know where my house is going to be."

COMMENTARY

Vicky is managing to cope with many family problems and frequent moves. She identifies many people who help her. Vicky's personality, which is outgoing and warm, makes it relatively easy for people to respond to her needs. She has the support of her grandmother, who helps her to figure out what is going on; her teacher, who understands and offers to talk with her; her friends, who like her; and the social workers, who help the family access financial assistance. Her stuffed animals provide comfort. Her capacity to think and talk about her family situation provides her with a way to explain things to herself. In situations that are scary for her, such as diving into deep water, Vicky takes some risks, jumps in, and "bounces back up."

T. J. also tries to cope by figuring out what has happened to his mother and family and how they ended up in a shelter. He reasons that his mother did the best she could, but that she also might need help. He has thought about homelessness in a way that makes the idea somewhat acceptable to him. His friends are a source of support. His music and his own room are a means of escape.

Homeless children experience significantly stressful life events. The most obvious stressful event is losing their home. Additionally, some of these children may have experienced separation from siblings or parents, violence or substance abuse in their family, or child abuse. In the face of these difficult circumstances, children and adolescents who are homeless, like most children, are remarkably resilient, surviving and getting on with life against the backdrop of considerable stress.

The stressors directly related to homelessness reflect two somewhat different sets of events: initially becoming homeless, and then remaining homeless. The major event of becoming homeless is clearly traumatic for any child. Months and years later, children can recall the small details of the day in which "we got homeless"—the landlord's demanding they move, the scene in court, the packing, the fleeing to a grandmother's crowded house, the bus ride across the country.

But while the fact of having become homeless always looms in the mind of the child, the greatest degree of stress may be caused by remaining homeless, that is, the chronic daily hassles of life in a shelter or motel. It is these day-to-day struggles and annoyances that weigh heavily on the lives of homeless children, and with which they must learn to cope.

Many would argue that homeless children should not have to learn to cope with circumstances that are so destructive—that a maladaptive response to such abnormal circumstances could, in itself, be a healthy reaction. Indeed, most mental health professionals do not find themselves working to help these children "adjust" to life in a shelter. Instead, these children are encouraged to express and constructively channel their frustrations, and to utilize any available resources that may help them to grow.

In dealing with the stresses of both homelessness and life in a shelter, children use a variety of strategies and coping mechanisms. In order merely to survive from day to day, many of these children must and do learn to manage the long-term and more immediate hassles. Some do not cope well. They may become severely withdrawn, or may act out excessively. Some only barely cope, struggling to keep it together. Their sadness and frustration are never far from the surface. Others have learned how to live through the experience fairly well and seem, at least on the face of things, to be reasonably well adjusted. These children are clearly aware of and in touch with the pain of their circumstances. However, they appear to be survivors and are driven to make it.

Like all children who must cope with stressful events, homeless children use two major kinds of coping strategies: those that directly address the problem and those that focus on the feelings resulting from the problem. Using problem-focused strategies, children and adolescents attempt to change the source of the problem—for example, "I'm going to get us out of this place. I'm going to beat on welfare" (Krissy). Using emotion-focused strategies, on the other hand, children attempt to manage their feelings about the problem, realizing at some level that the source of the problem cannot be changed—for example, "When I get sad about being here, I just go outside and try to find some kids to play with" (Claire). These two types of strategies are used to cope with the event of becoming homeless as well as with the day-to-day hassles of shelter living.

Coping with the Event of Homelessness

Most of the time, children do not try to solve the problem of homelessness directly. They are aware at some level that because the event has already occurred, they are no longer in a position to prevent it, and because they are children, they do not have the power to change it. Older children and adolescents are particularly aware of the futility of such attempts. They realize that the events that brought them to the shelter and the activities necessary to get out of the shelter and to move into permanent housing are well beyond their control. Adolescents are more likely than younger children to perceive the complexity of the situation and to know that no easy solution exists.

Younger children and preschoolers, in a Don Quixote-like manner, do make occasional stabs at changing the source of the problem and getting rid of the homelessness. Some make this attempt by trying to get some control, that is, acting as if they were the parent. When going to visit potential apartments with their mothers, they evaluate the pluses and minuses of the apartment with an adult-like shrewdness: "Well the place didn't have enough bedrooms. We'd be too crowded there, I know we would" (Susan); or "The place is pretty good. The furniture was good. We'd have to get chairs and rugs though. But we should take it" (Robert). Some even try to manage the mother's application for subsidized housing: "I keep telling her to hurry up and fill out them papers. We need to get out of here" (Lori).

Others propose solutions that reflect the magical thinking of this age group. Some, for example, collect their pennies to help their mother pay for an apartment, while another may tell her to move to an empty house the child happened to notice on a nearby street.

But even young children do not spend much of their energy trying to change the source of the problem of becoming homeless. Instead, children and adolescents attempt to deal with the emotions that result from their becoming homeless. Children have a variety of coping mechanisms, often reflective of their age.

A strategy that children frequently rely on to cope with their painful feelings about having become homeless involves constructing an explanation for themselves about why they became homeless, that is, by intellectually or cognitively restructuring the event. In younger children, these restructured accounts are often unrealistic or magical tales, attributing the cause of their homelessness to some external event unrelated to their parents or themselves. "People needed our house. They had no place to live. So we goed out" (David).

Some older children are more likely to restructure the event by almost explaining away what they perceive to be the real cause of their homelessness, particularly if they perceive the real cause to be a parent. While children may initially suggest the parent's habits, for example, drugs, poor management skills, or lifestyle, as reasons for the homeless-ness, some immediately try to account for these parental behaviors. Rather than conclude that these actions reflect what they assume would look like the parent's lack of love for them, some children offer reasons for the parent's past and present behavior. These explanations are not usually excuses for that behavior, but a way for them to talk to themselves about it and live with it. Some conclude their parents might be "sick" or "have problems." Ian traces his mother's "mistakes" and "problems," many of which contributed to his inadequate nurturance, back to her own history of abuse. Tucker, who believes his family is repeatedly homeless because his mother doesn't know how to manage their money, says that she spends too much on the children, "trying to make us too happy." In some confusing way, Tucker concludes, she loves them too much.

Other children do not try to rationalize their parents' behavior, but cope with it by differentiating themselves from it. They make it clear that they would not choose the same path as their parents. They attribute their homelessness ultimately to their status as children who must comply with their parents' wishes. They describe themselves as powerless to do anything about the condition in which they find themselves, even though they resent some of what they perceive to be the choices that their parents have made, for example, repeated moving. In trying to explain how they cope with a family announcement of another move, children often invoke their status as children who must be obedient to their parents. "We have to move because my mom says. We say no and she says yes" (Kelly). "If your mom says it, then you got to do it" (Curt). As they see it, obedience is the bottom line if they are to survive.

Even though they may be disappointed with their parents' behavior, many children survive by maintaining an unswerving hope that this behavior will change. Often this hope is based on their previous experience, in which things did improve, if only temporarily. There are a number of families for whom the shelter is a transitional residence between drug or alcohol rehabilitation programs and living on their own again. Children in these families have hope that the changes and improvements that their parents have made will be lasting.

Some children cope with being homeless by redefining the word "homelessness" so that it means something more acceptable to them. T. J. does this when he states that it is better to call the shelter your home than to say you don't know where your home is or will be. Jose, who is twelve, asserted that his friend "knows that I live here because I'm new around here."

Some children cope by engaging in wishful thinking. They hope that the next house will be better and fantasize about how it might look. Jose, a boy whose family has moved many times, still envisioned the next house as being better, but protected himself against disappointment by concluding that any house is better than the shelter.

> I like moving a lot because when you find a different house it's going to be a nice one instead of the other ones, the other houses. The other houses were only kind of good. A nice house is pretty. It's nice from inside and outside. I used to live in a house that was not nice. But if it's an ugly house I still say nice because I like a house. A house is better than being here. I wish I could go to a house. I like living here, but sometimes I go here and sometimes I want to go home.

Coping with Chronic Daily Stressors

Without doubt, the fact of homelessness is a major stressful event in the lives of homeless children. Additionally, other major life stressors, such as family violence or abuse, intensify the burden of many homeless children. However, on a day-to-day basis, the hassles of shelter living are what makes the greatest demands on the coping skills of these children.

The sources of the stress are many, resulting mostly from having to live for a long period of time in a very small space, in close proximity to strangers, in circumstances over which the child and his or her parent have very little control. Petty annoyances can become unbearable for these children in a situation in which they feel trapped. The food may not be what one is used to or likes, other children and families may make too much noise, particularly at night. The television may be too loud, or too soft, or on the wrong channel, or controlled by someone else. There may be no place to play, no place to be alone, no protection for one's belongings, few toys, few friends, and too many bothersome little kids. People in the shelter—staff and clients—are strangers, and often are different from the kind of friends one might choose, in both interpersonal style and personal habits.

School is new and different, and often not perceived as welcoming "shelter kids." Homework is difficult to start or finish in noisy, crowded surroundings. Most critically, all the familiar people and personal belongings from pre-shelter days are simply not there. The process of getting out is long, complicated, and uncertain. It is with many or some of these stressors that children must continuously cope while in the shelter. To survive and manage, children use a variety of strategies.

In trying to deal with the daily hassles of shelter living, some children use problem-focused strategies, often with minimal success. These strategies attempt to change the source of the problem, which often is, by its nature, unchangeable. To manage his frustration about not being able to watch his favorite TV program, Pedro appointed himself to be "in charge of the channel we watched." The other guests at the shelter moved with dispatch to quash his plan. Through experiences like this one, children quickly come to realize that trying to alter the source of frustrations in a group living situation is nearly impossible. Consequently, children are most likely to utilize emotion-focused coping strategies, through which they try to address and manage a range of painful feelings, from frustration and sadness to anger and depression.

Preschool children do not have well-developed coping strategies, and often respond to the tension and stress of the shelter by regressing in a number of domains. The literature is replete with examples of young homeless children whose development of cognitive skills, such as language or perceptual-motor functioning, is delayed. Some young children develop behavior problems, manifested as either acting out, or becoming withdrawn, or regressing to earlier ways of behaving, for example, bed wetting or night terrors.

As children get older, they widen the range of their coping skills. School-aged children and adolescents have a number of strategies for surviving in the shelter. Some children manage to cope by looking at the shelter not in terms of its problems and flaws, but in terms of the good things that the shelter provides. Children can often describe what are to them one or two major advantages of living in the shelter. "This motel is real good because we have a swimming pool here" (Gary). "I like it here a lot because the school bus drops me off and picks me up right at the front door" (Ryan).

Others cope by developing strong attachments to other people in the shelter: staff, other parents, or children. Some have ongoing and strong relationships with grandparents or other relatives in their extended families. The social support generated by these relationships fortifies children's inner strength. Some children become good friends with one or another of the shelter workers. In situations where there is not an overwhelming number of children, staff members are able to develop individual relationships with these children, which provide them with considerable support. "My favorite person here is Chris. She showed me her homework from college. She goes to college and works here. She gave me a pencil to do homework that I get from school. I think she likes me best of all too" (Tara).

Some school-aged children make friends with other children in the shelter, or, on rare occasions, with children in school who may live at another shelter in the area. At this age, children who are homeless understand each other's plight and sometimes talk with each other about the difficult circumstances of the shelter. Developing a closeness to other homeless children is more likely to occur in large shelters where there are a number of children of similar ages. Meeting children in similar situations provides children with someone who understands. "My friend Tracey lives in a shelter too. We found out by accident one day. It's good because she knows how I feel and I know how she feels" (Ingrid).

Older children and adolescents often receive support from friends outside the shelter, either friends from their old neighborhood or school, or if they are new to the area, friends whom they have made in school since moving to the shelter. Most adolescents have a few friends to whom they are able to talk about their current situation and who provide them with sympathetic support. Ian, for example, stated:

I have other friends I can talk to when I'm upset about something. I talk with anybody really. Any of my friends. Sometimes when I get upset, I can talk to my mother. Sometimes. But that's hard because some things you just don't talk to your mother about. My stepfather too, he's not the kind that talks. He's not the kind of type that goes out with a lot of girls.

Children also cope by constantly reminding themselves that they are waiting for a house and that the house will come. Shelter staff and parents reinforce these beliefs by discussing various aspects of acquiring housing, such as filling out the necessary forms. Once the approval for subsidized housing has been obtained, children often go with parents to look for an apartment, and return with hope, if not a home. Other children and families who have been in the shelter longer are seen moving out. In spite of months and months of waiting, all of this concrete evidence sustains hope.

A small number of children are able to cope by expressing their sad or angry feelings quite directly. They talk with their parents, with staff, or other adults in the shelter. Most, though, are reluctant to bring up their feelings, knowing that their mother may feel the same way or that the staff person may take offense at their feelings. It is difficult, as these children see it, to bite the hand that feeds them. If one complains about a situation that is, at the moment, "better than nothing," then you might indeed be left with nothing.

Other children find themselves unable to express their feelings to anyone. These children describe "getting real down" and do not seem to have solutions for managing the depression. While these children do not deny the feelings when the subject is raised, they do not share them spontaneously with anyone else on a regular basis. Juan clearly asserted, "I don't like to talk about this stuff." Haydn similarly said, "I keep everything to myself. If I want to tell, it's only like if I think it's the right time to say something and I've been holding it in for a while. Then I say something. But otherwise, I don't say anything."

Some children, particularly if the family is religious, try to manage by praying for a miracle. They are hopeful that God will get them out of the shelter and find them a house. Sean described asking God to help him find a house, and reported that "God says, 'You'll find one.' "

Bringing their favorite toy to the shelter makes the transition easier for some younger children. Toys are often children's most important possessions. They provide a sense of security, particularly when children are anxious. Vicky managed to bring several of her stuffed animals, and finds these comforting. While some children may not have their toys with them, they know where they are temporarily stored and how they can be recovered. "My toys are at my nana's and I'm going to get them when we get a house" (Sarah). In the process of moving, some children may completely lose their toys, and are deeply saddened by this loss.

For a small number of children, their investment in and excitement about their life, work, and friends at school constitute a major source of support and positive feelings. School provides these children with a place that is completely separate from the shelter and in which they can be, for a few hours a day, "just like everyone else. Being like everyone else usually means keeping their homelessness and current shelter address completely secret. Younger children, particularly, become absorbed in the activities of school and the life of the classroom. "I like my teacher and I'm learning how to read. Mommy's going to buy me a book. And I'm going to go to school every day. I'm never going to be sick" (Matt). As they become older, children who have managed to remain academically competent maintain their investment in school and use this as a major coping strategy. Some even begin to plan their future around their academic achievements. Unfortunately, many children who are homeless do not have a positive school experience, gradually lose interest in school, and no longer find school a way to cope with shelter living.

For some children, fantasy becomes an important way to cope with the pain of shelter living. Reading books is one source of escape, particularly for school-aged girls. A number of these young girls describe how they deal with their angry or sad feelings by escaping with a book. Many children spend long periods in front of the TV watching what they describe as their "favorite program"—cartoons. As they become lost in the world of fantasy, they become momentarily oblivious to the noise, chaos, and frustration of the shelter.

Other children use fantasy play to express their painful feelings. Ryan, who is twelve and has moved around the country many times, has brought his set of Ninja Turtle toy figures to the shelter and plays with them constantly. This usually depressed and uncommunicative boy becomes animated when describing the world of the turtles. In his play, one can hear the pain that he himself has experienced. Pointing to one of the figures, he said:

This guy here, he was the leader of the foot soldiers when he was a person. And this guy was his best ninja and he turned against him and forced him to move to America. They threw him out of Japan into America. It wasn't fair either. And he couldn't get anyone to like him when he came to America. He had to live in the sewers. His only friends was the rats in the sewers. And he got slime dumped on him by this guy from the Mansion X. He feels pretty bad about getting kicked out and having to go to America, pretty bad.

After a brief time in the shelter, children become keenly aware of the lack of control in their lives. They realize their powerlessness to do anything about the circumstances in which they find themselves. Imagining a future when they will be in control often helps them to endure the present situation. They imagine a time when they will be in charge, and describe how they will do things to protect others from the fate they currently know. As one little boy boasted, "Pretty soon no one in my family's going to have to worry. I'm going to take care of them, get a job. I'll make a hundred dollars and buy a house" (Paul). Stephanie, who is ten and seldom sees her sisters and her mother, who is separated from her father, stated: "When I get big, I'm going to go to Georgia to see my sister and then get a job."

Ultimately, what sustains these children is hope. They are remarkable survivors. In spite of overwhelming circumstances and repeated disappointments, they have not given up on the world. They are always hoping for better days, either in the immediate or distant future. One eight-year-old concretized the hope: "When I get sad I keep remembering to myself that it's going to get better. The shelter is just for a little while. I know it will be better. I just know it" (David).

Chapter Twelve

Conclusion

As children almost always will, these children tell their stories with a near brutal honesty. Some are blunt, as Ian was when he declares unequivocally, "I hate living here." Others are more understated, as is Elizabeth when she told her school chum, "Being homeless isn't no fun." But rarely do these children make efforts to hide their pain, or to cloak it in words that are easier for adults to hear. They tell of the world of homelessness as they feel it and see it. As Haydn described his awareness of a difficult family situation, they have "seen and know what [they've] seen." While they are relieved not to be living on the streets, they do not try to justify the experience of the shelter. Without ambivalence, every single one of them insists that having a home is better. In collecting the stories in this volume, there was no way to temper the sadness, fear, and anger that they reveal. These stories stand as naked testimony to the effects of homelessness on the fragile young lives of these children.

The stories tell of a sense of identity that is assaulted by the loss of one's home. Home is where a person can be most who he or she is. The profound significance of homelessness for children or adults lies in the loss of a fundamental organizing structure in their lives. "Personal place" is a central contributor to one's sense of identity (Rivlin, 1986). To lose one's home is to become disconnected from a part of oneself. For children, who are in the process of developing a sense of who they are, such a disruption can be devastating. In some senses, becoming homeless leaves children without the ground under their feet. As they tell it in their

stories, "the worst part of the living in a shelter is not being able to feel
that you're 'at home' " (Juan).

Homelessness and poverty have robbed these children of a good part
of their childhood. They have been forced to worry about the things that
most children take for granted—food, safety, and a roof over their heads.
Some become "little adults" in their efforts to help themselves and their
families to survive. And yet, as their stories remind us, they are children.
They cherish their toys, they play at the hint of any opportunity, they
rush to get lost in the world of fantasy. They think in the magical and
concrete ways of children, constructing their world with the logic of
childhood. And they make clear in their stories that they would like to
be treated as children—to be less burdened by worry and more able to
depend on adults for the basics of survival. As one adolescent described
it, "For a long time now, I've been a grown-up and a kid at the same
time" (Mary).

Ultimately, these stories are as much about poverty as homelessness.
As these children tell it, the burden of poverty is not simply the lack of
material possessions. It means facing full square the psychological and
social ills that accompany poverty in our society. These children confront
family dysfunction, substance abuse, and violence. They have known
poor schooling, inadequate medical care, and substandard housing. They
experience the frustration resulting from a lack of resources to help them
and a lack of opportunity in the larger society to make things better. Some
sense the generations of hopelessness in their own families that have kept
them moving in search of a better life. They know a society that, in some
corners, is inclined to believe that they are poor because they choose to
be. They have an acute awareness of the shame of poverty and the
degradation resulting from society's moral judgments of the poor.
Ultimately, their pain is their utter powerlessness—as children and as
poor people—to do anything about the fate that has befallen them.

In this context of pain and struggle, the stories also reveal an
extraordinary capacity for survival in difficult circumstances. When
describing how they or other homeless children manage to get through
the experience, the children often use the phrase "I make the best of
it." Haydn said that other children who become homeless should "look
on the bright side of things," even though he confessed he didn't know
exactly what that bright side is. In spite of their fundamental discontent,
many children manage to find some redeeming feature of the shelter.
When the motel has nothing by way of amenities, they enthuse about
the swimming pool. When the shelter offers only food and a roof, they
are happy that their room is close to the kitchen so that they can get

snacks. When they are looking forward to months in a crowded room, they get excited about the "free clothes from donations." Their optimism doesn't lessen their pain, but it keeps them going from one day to the next.

The stories also reveal these children's hopes for the future. They have not given up, and find themselves continuing to wish and often to believe that things will get better. Many are able to imagine a happier life for themselves, either in the immediate future or when they get to be adults. Like all children, they nurture their dreams for what and who they might be. But unlike most children, their dreams are not casual and often-changing wishes, but rather the stuff of their souls, which keeps them going.

Some dream about their future lives as adults. After living in a series of substandard apartments, and finally landing in a shelter, Juan shared little but sadness and pain. Finally, his face lit up as he talked about his tomorrow. "I want to go to the academy for high school and I think I can because I'm smart in eighth grade. I get straight A's. And then, I want to go to Harvard or Yale. My big brother told me about this and it's what I want to do." Kendra said she wants to be an actress. "I've always wanted to be an actress. I like to be in plays and I like to sing. I can sing pretty good. . . . I want to sing, I really want to sing. I want to sing and I want to act and that's my main goal."

Others dream about making their present life better. Troy wanted

a good life, a basketball trophy and a nice house. In a good life, everything goes right for you. You don't have to live on welfare or anything. . . . And life would be good if you could never be worried. . . . that anything might happen to you like die from an overdose. I want a basketball trophy. I play every position. I don't have my own basketball. I had one but somebody here stuck a needle into it. And I want a nice house. It would be clean and just be a cool house.

Elizabeth wanted "a lot of things like money in my family, a house and a good future and I want that we won't have to come back to the shelter anymore."

Dana is working to change his present life as a means for having a better future. Formerly involved in inner-city gangs, Dana has now resolved that

I'm not even going to hang around with those gang kids anymore. The only person I hang around with is my friend Kip. And Kip ain't all about that. Getting into gangs, he's not about that. He's about going to college, getting an education. He's not about being a bum and stuff like that. . . . And we all made up what we going to do. Go to college and become somebody. I want to go to UNLV. In school I'm doing great. Usually I'm getting A's, B's, and C's. When I was in the city I was getting straight F's.

In their stories, these children often unknowingly, offer clear suggestions for how adults might help them. They ask that we understand their ambivalent feelings about living in a shelter. They want us to know that their complaints are not meant to be heard as a lack of appreciation for the roof over their heads. It is not the efforts of the shelter staff that are the subject of their complaints but the very fact of having lost their home and having to live in this or any shelter. They grumble about "the rotten food" or "the lady in charge" because it is less painful than reminding themselves of what has happened to them.

They ask that, as helping professionals, we not judge them. They are terrified of being labeled as poor and homeless, because they know that so often, poor means "bad." Tara is sure that her teacher yells at her because her family is on welfare. In their stories, they ask us to remember that they are innocent victims who have no choice. As Haydn pointedly asserted, "I didn't ask to come here."

As young as some of these children are, they ask the adults who work with them to honor their trust. It is critically important to them that the adults who know of their plight protect their confidentiality. Most, for example, are willing and even want to have their teacher know about their difficult circumstances, but worry that the teacher might tell. "My teacher might tell another teacher who might tell some kids," and the dreaded word that they are "homeless" would spread among their peers. The taunting and derision that they assume would result terrifies these children.

They ask that we respect their privacy, while not leaving them alone. They clearly assert their right to be in charge of when they tell what to whom. But they also don't want us to ignore the place they are coming from or pretend that it does not exist. Helping professionals have a delicate balancing act with these or any children—to respond to their sometimes obscure invitation to come into their lives, yet at the same time to avoid crossing the threshold without an invitation. The children are ambivalent about the telling and look for a clue that the other wants to listen, but will not pressure them to do so. Haydn, in telling his story and expressing his feelings, said he chooses not to talk about his feelings: "I just keep them trapped inside." He sees himself as similar to his brother Dana, who is also "quiet about those things. He doesn't say anything about it"—but "if you ask him, he'll tell you."

Even though they do not articulate it very clearly, homeless children also ask for reassurance that they are not alone. They want and need to recognize their struggle as one that is shared in different ways by many children and families. They respond with eager curiosity when helping professionals point out that other kids have these worries too. Seeing their problems against the backdrop of the common human struggle helps them to relieve the loneliness with which their circumstances have surrounded them.

As they risk telling their stories, they hope against hope that helping professionals will not react in horror and walk away from hearing more. At some level, they sense that if adults do not get shocked by their story, then they do not have to get shocked by it either. To be "blown away" or suddenly break contact with them, in their eyes, is to judge them. After April "told everything" to a guidance counselor who said "We'll meet again," April recounted with obvious disappointment and sadness, "we never met again."

They ask that we educate children and adults about who homeless families really are. These children are heavily burdened by what they see as society's negative perception of the homeless. In their stories, they take significant pains to point out that other families they meet in the shelter are "nice people." In their childlike way, they would like the world to know that people in the shelter "are nice people just like us."

Particularly when they are older, they are clear about asking helping professionals and other adults to advocate for the needs of homeless children and families. Tucker is very specific in his recommendation that if he were going to tell grown-ups what it's like for a kid to be homeless, he would tell them "that it's not very good . . . if they're rich they should help a lot."

Finally, they ask helping professionals to recognize the worth of their stories and the value of their lives. While most children are embarrassed about so many aspects of their lives, and tell their stories only to those whom they trust, they often express a pride about being able to disclose what is in the heart of a homeless child and family. At the end of his story, when he was again being reassured that his identity would be kept confidential, Tucker suddenly insisted, "Go ahead and tell them my name so I could be proud." While the identity of every child who told their story has been protected, Tucker's pride is clearly evident. He claims for all of these children a pride that the stories they have told with such honesty will assist helping professionals to better serve homeless children and ultimately contribute to the eradication of homelessness.

References

Acker, P. J., Fierman, A. H., & Dreyer, B. P. (1987). An assessment of parameters of health care and nutrition in homeless children. *American Journal of Disabled Children*, *141*, 388.

Alperstein, G., & Arnstein, E. (1988). Homeless children: A challenge for pediatricians. *The Pediatric Clinics of North America*, *35*(6), 1413–1425.

Alperstein, G., Rappaport, C., & Flanigan, J. M. (1988). Health problems of homeless children in New York City. *American Journal of Public Health*, *78*(9), 1232–1233.

Axelson, L. J., & Dail, P. W. (1988). The changing character of homelessness in the United States. *Family Relations*, *37*, 463–469.

Bassuk, E. L. (Ed.) (1986). *The mental health needs of homeless persons: New directions for mental health services*. San Francisco: Jossey-Bass.

Bassuk, E. L. (1987). The feminization of homelessness: Families in Boston shelters. *American Journal of Social Psychiatry*, *7*(1), 19–23.

Bassuk, E. L. (1990). The problem of family homelessness. In E. L. Bassuk, R. W. Carman, & L. Weinreb (Eds.), *Community care for homeless families: A program design manual* (pp. 7–12). Washington, DC: Interagency Council on the Homeless.

Bassuk, E. L., Carman, R. W., & Weinreb, L. F. (1990). *Community care for homeless families: A program design manual*. Washington, DC: Interagency Council on the Homeless.

Bassuk, E. L., & Gallagher, E. M. (1990). The impact of homelessness on children. *Child and Youth Services*, *14*(1), 19–33.

Bassuk, E. L., & Lauriat, A. (1986). Are emergency shelters the solution? *International Journal of Mental Health, 14*(4), 72–97.

Bassuk, E. L., & Rosenberg, L. (1988). Why does family homelessness occur? A case-control study. *American Journal of Public Health, 78*(7), 783–788.

Bassuk, E. L., & Rubin, L. (1987). Homeless children: A neglected population. *American Journal of Orthopsychiatry, 57*(2), 279–286.

Bassuk, E. L., Rubin, L., & Lauriat, A. (1986). Characteristics of sheltered homeless families. *American Journal of Public Health, 76*(9), 1097–1101.

Berezin, J. (1988) *Promises to keep: Child care for New York City's homeless children.* New York: Child Care, Inc.

Bibace, R., & Walsh, M. E. (1979). Clinical developmental psychologists in family practice settings. *Professional Psychology, 10,* 441–450.

Bibace, R., & Walsh, M. E. (1981). *Children's conceptions of health, illness and bodily functions. New directions in developmental psychology series.* San Francisco: Jossey-Bass.

Bingham, R. D., Green, R. E., & White, S. B. (1987). *The homeless in contemporary society.* Newbury Park, CA: Sage.

Boxill, N., & Beatty, A. (1990). Mother/child interaction among homeless women and their children in a public night shelter in Atlanta, Georgia. *Child and Youth Services, 14*(1), 49–64.

Breakey, W. R., & Fischer, P. J. (1990). Homelessness: The extent of the problem. *Journal of Social Issues, 46*(4), 31–47.

Bruner, J. S. (1990). *Acts of Meaning.* Cambridge, MA: Harvard University Press.

Bureau of the Census, U.S. Department of Commerce. (1985). *Current population reports: characteristics of the population below the poverty level.* Washington, DC: Government Printing Office.

Burt, M. R., & Cohen, B. E. (1989). Differences among homeless single women, women with children, and single men. *Social Problems, 36*(5), 508–523.

Center for Law and Education. (1987, September). Homelessness: A barrier to education for thousands of children. *Newsnotes, 38,* 1–2.

Chavkin, W., Kristal, A., Seabron, C., & Guigli, P. E. (1987). Reproductive experience of women living in hotels for the homeless in New York City. *New York State Journal of Medicine, 87,* 10–13.

Children's Defense Fund. (1988). *The children's defense budget: An analysis of our nation's investment in children.* Washington, DC: Children's Defense Fund.

Citizens Committee for Children of New York. (1984). *1000 homeless children: The crisis continues: The third report on homeless families with children in temporary shelter.* New York: Citizens Committee for Children of New York.

Citizens Committee for Children. (1988). *Children in storage: Families in New York City's barracks-style shelters.* New York: Citizens Committee for Children.

Coles, R. (1989). *The call of stories.* Boston: Houghton Mifflin.

Colorado Children's Campaign. (1987). *No room at the inn: A study of Colorado's homeless parents and children: Who are they, why are they homeless, what can be done?* Denver: Colorado Children's Campaign.

Damrosch, S., Sullivan, P., Scholler, A., & Gaines, J. (1988). On behalf of homeless families. *Maternal Child Nursing, 13,* 259–263.

Dobbin, M. (1987, August 3). The children of the homeless. *U.S. News and World Report,* 19–21.

Dubowitz, H., Newberger, C., Melnicoe, L. & Newberger, E. (1988). The changing American family. *The Pediatric Clinics of North America,* 35(6), 1291–1311.

Eddowes, E. A., & Hranitz, J. R. (1989). Educating children of the homeless. *Childhood Education, 65*(4), 197–200.

Edelman, M. W., & Mihaly, L. (1989). Homeless families and the housing crisis in the United States. *Children and Youth Services Review, 11,* 91–108.

Gallagher, E. (1986). *No place like home.* Boston, MA: Massachusetts Committee for Children and Youth.

Gewirtzman, R., & Fodor, I. (1987). The homeless child at school: From welfare hotel to classroom. *Child Welfare, 66*(3), 237–245.

Grant, R. (1989). *Assessing the damage: The impact of shelter experience on homeless young children.* New York: Association to Benefit Children.

Hall, J. A., & Maza, P. L. (1990). No fixed address; The effects of homelessness on families and children. *Child and Youth Services, 14*(1), 35–47.

Haus, A. (Ed.) (1988). *Working with homeless people: A guide for staff and volunteers.* New York: Columbia University Community Services.

Henry Street Settlement. (1987). *Training program for shelter managers, staff and volunteers.* New York: Henry Street Settlement.

Homeless Information Exchange. (1988). *Family and child homelessness.* Washington, DC: Homeless Information Exchange.

Horowitz, S. V., Springer, C. M., & Kose, G. (1988). Stress in hotel children: The effects of homelessness on attitudes toward school. *Children's Environments Quarterly, 5*(1), 34–36.

Hutchinson, W. J., Searight, P., & Stretch, J. J. (1986). Multidimensional networking: A response to the needs of homeless families. *Social Work, 31*(6), 427–430.

Johnson, A. K., & Kreuger, L. W. (1989). Toward a better understanding of homeless women. *Social Work, 34*(6), 537–540.

Knickman, J. R., & Weitzman, B. C. (1989). *A study of homeless families in New York City: Risk assessment models and strategies for prevention.* Final report, vol. 1. New York: New York University.

Kozol, J. (1987). *Rachel and her children: Homeless families in America.* New York: Crown Publishers.

Kronenfeld, D., Phillips, M., & Middleton-Jeter, V. (1978-1980). *The forgotten ones: Treatment of single parent multi-problem families in a residential setting.* Washington, DC: U.S. Department of Health and Human Services. (Grant Number 18-P-90705/03f.)

Lewis, M. R., & Meyers, A. F. (1989). The growth and development status of homeless children entering shelters in Boston. *Public Health Reports, 104*(3), 247-250.

Lindsey, A. M. (1989). Health care for the homeless. *Nursing Outlook, 37*(2), 78-81.

Long, L. A. (1988). *Helping homeless families: A training curriculum.* Long Island City, NY: La Guardia Community College.

McChesney, K. Y. (1990). Family homelessness: A systemic problem. *Journal of Social Issues, 46*(4), 191-205.

Massachusetts Department of Education. (1988). *Report on the education of homeless children in Massachusetts.* Quincy, MA: Office of the Education of Homeless Children and Youth.

Maza, P. L., & Hall, J. A. (1987). *Study of homeless children and families: Preliminary findings.* Washington, DC: Child Welfare League of America and Traveler's Aid International.

Miller, D. S., & Lin, E. (1988). Children in sheltered homeless families: Reported health status and use of health services. *Pediatrics, 81*(5), 668-673.

Mills, C., & Ota, H. (1989). Homeless women with minor children in the Detroit metropolitan area. *Social Work, 34*(6), 485-489.

Molnar, J. (1988). *Home is where the heart is: The crisis of homeless children and families in New York City.* New York: Bank Street College of Education.

Molnar, J., Hartman, A., & Klein T. (1988). *Transitional shelters for homeless families: Early childhood component.* New York: Bank Street College of Education.

Molnar, J. M., & Rath, W. R. (1990). Constantly compromised: The impact of homelessness on children. *Journal of Social Issues, 46*(4), 109-124.

National Alliance to End Homelessness. (1988). *Housing and homelessness.* Washington, DC: National Alliance to End Homelessness.

National Alliance to End Homelessness. (1990). *Checklist for success: Programs to help the hungry and homeless.* Alexandria, VA: Emergency Food and Shelter National Board.

National Coalition for the Homeless. (1984). *Perchance to sleep: Homeless children without shelter in New York City.* New York: National Coalition for the Homeless.

National Coalition for the Homeless. (1987a). *Broken lives: Denial of education to homeless children.* Washington, DC: National Coalition for the Homeless.

National Coalition for the Homeless. (1987b). *Homelessness in the United States: Background and federal response.* Washington, DC: National Coalition for the Homeless.

National Coalition for the Homeless. (1988). *Over the edge: Homeless families and the welfare system.* Washington, DC: National Coalition for the Homeless.

National Resource Center on Homelessness and Mental Illness. (1990). *Working with homeless children at risk for severe emotional disturbance.* Delmar, NY: National Resource Center on Homelessness and Mental Illness.

Neiman, L. (1988). A critical review of resiliency literature and its relevance to homeless children. *Children's Environment Quarterly, 5*(1), 17–25.

Phillips, M., DeChillo, N., Kronenfeld, D., & Middleton-Jeter, V. (1988). Homeless families: Services make a difference. *Social Case Work, 69*(11), 48–53.

Rafferty, Y., & Rollins, N. (1989). *Learning in limbo: The educational deprivation of homeless children.* New York: Advocates for Children.

Reyes, L. M., & Waxman, L. D. (1986). *The continued growth of hunger, homelessness and poverty in America's cities: 1986.* Washington, DC: U.S. Conference of Mayors.

Rivlin, L. (1986). A new look at the homeless. *Social Policy, 16*(4), 3–10.

Rivlin, L. G. (1990a). Home and homelessness in the lives of children. *Child and Youth Services, 14*(1), 5–17.

Rivlin, L. G. (1990b). The significance of home and homelessness. *Marriage and Family Review, 15*(1–2), 39–56.

Roberts, L., & Henry M. (1986, July–August). State ordered to shelter homeless families. *Youth Law News,* 1–3.

Rosenman, M., & Stein, M. L. (1990). Homeless children: A new vulnerability. *Child and Youth Services, 14*(1), 89–109.

Russell, S. C., & Williams, E. U. (1988). Homeless handicapped children: A special education perspective. *Children's Environments Quarterly, 5*(1), 3–7.

Shinn, M., Knickman, J. R., Ward, D., Petrovic, N. L., & Muth, B. J. (1990). Alternative models for sheltering homeless families. *Journal of Social Issues, 46*(4), 175–190.

Shinn, M., & Weitzman, B. C. (1990). Research on homelessness: An introduction. *Journal of Social Issues, 46*(4), 1–11.

Solarz, A., & Bogat, G. A. (1990). When social support fails: The homeless. *Journal of Community Psychology, 18*(1), 79–96.

Sprague, J. F. (1988). Taking action: *A comprehensive approach to housing women and children in Massachusetts.* Boston: Women's Institute for Housing and Economic Development.

Stewart B. McKinney Homeless Assistance Act. Public Law 100-77 (7/22/87), codified at 42 U.S.C. SS11301-11472.

Stretch, J. J., Kreuger, L. W., Johnson, A. K., & Hutchinson, W. J. (1988). *The homeless continuum model serving homeless families.* St. Louis, MO: Salvation Army.

U.S. Conference of Mayors. (1988). *A status report on children in America's cities: A 52-page survey.* Washington, DC: U.S. Conference of Mayors.

U.S. House of Representatives Select Committee on Children, Youth and Families. (1987). *The crisis in homelessness: Effects on children and families.* Washington, DC: U.S. Government Printing Office.

Vermund, S. H., Belmar, R., & Drucker, E. (1987). Homelessness in New York City: The youngest victims. *New York State Journal of Medicine, 87*(1), 3-5.

Walsh, M. E. (1990, August). Psychosocial functioning in homeless and poor housed families. Paper presented at symposium, Public Interest Miniconvention—Homelessness: Community Research, Action and Agenda for Public Policy. Ninety-eighth annual meeting of the American Psychological Association, Boston, MA.

Waxman, L. D., & Reyes, L. M. (1987). *A status report on homeless families in America's cities: A 29-city survey.* Washington, DC: U.S. Conference of Mayors.

Waxman, L. D., & Reyes, L. M. (1989). *A status report on hunger and homelessness in America's cities: 1988.* Washington, DC: U.S. Conference of Mayors.

Weinreb, L. F., & Bassuk, E. L. (1990). Substance abuse: A growing problem among homeless families. *Family and Community Health, 13*(1), 55-64.

Weitzman, B. C., Knickman, J. R., & Shinn, M. (1990). Pathways to homelessness among New York City families. *Journal of Social Issues, 46*(4), 125-140.

Women and Housing Task Force. (1990). *Unlocking the door: An action program for meeting the housing needs of women.* Washington, DC: National Low Income Housing Coalition.

Wood, D., Schlossman, S., Hayashi, T., & Valdez, R. (1989). *Over the brink: Homeless families in Los Angeles.* Los Angeles, CA: Assembly Office of Research.

Wright, J. D. (1990). Poor people, poor health: The health status of the homeless. *Journal of Social Issues, 46*(4), 49-64.

Wright, J. D., & Weber, E. (1987). *Homelessness and health.* New York: McGraw-Hill.

Index

About the Author

MARY E. WALSH is Associate Professor and Director of the Doctoral Training Program in Counseling Psychology in the School of Education at Boston College. She is an Adjunct Associate Professor in the Department of Family and Community Medicine at the University of Massachusetts Medical School. She is the co-author of *Children's Conceptions of Health, Illness, and Bodily Functions* as well as the author of numerous scholarly and professional journal articles.